**Comhairle Contae Thiobraid**
Tipperary County Council
Library Service

www.tipperarycoco.ie   076 1066 100

Items should be returned on or before the last date shown below.
Items can be renewed by phone, online or at your local library.

DATE DUE	DATE DUE	DATE DUE
TEMPLEMORE 0504 32555		

THE
GREEN
COOKBOOK

For Alba

RUKMINI IYER

THE
GREEN
COOKBOOK

EASY VEGAN & VEGETARIAN DINNERS

 SQUARE PEG

INTRODUCTION

At the end of a working day, I want a minimum effort, maximum flavour family dinner, as hassle-free as possible while still feeling like there's something joyous on our plates. For the last few years and through the *Roasting Tin* cookbooks, this has involved sticking all my ingredients into one tin and letting the oven do the work. While there are still plenty of one-tin options here, with cost and fuel-efficiency in mind I wanted to include more than just roasting-tin dinners – I want this to be a cookbook you can turn to Monday through Sunday for everything from 15-minute pasta ideas and budget-friendly batch-cooking to celebratory feasts for friends. Ideal for flexitarians, vegetarians, vegans and those looking for gluten-free meal solutions, this book is packed with recipes for when you get home from work and are tempted to order a Deliveroo but realise you can pull together ridiculously moreish miso butter noodles with tomatoes & spring onions (page 26) in 12 minutes instead. Or, if you've spent a day with the children and need to get their dinner on the table while they're occupied with a bowl of halved grapes and a few episodes of *Bluey*, you might try something from the Family Dinners chapter (pages 90–125) for that elusive unicorn of a dish, one that both the children and adults in your household can sit and eat together. If you're having friends round and want to put a big pot of food on the table, there's a whole chapter for that, too, and if you've got an entire hour free to batch-cook for the week ahead, you might try the one-pot pasta with peppers & harissa (page 190) or the crispy leek, cheddar & mustard loaded potatoes (page 186), which freeze beautifully (I was particularly grateful for a freezer bag of these when my husband and I got home from the hospital after our daughter Alba's birth).

I'm a pescatarian, but by far our weeknight dinners are plant-led or plant-based, and feedback from readers of the *Roasting Tin* books suggests that you're here because you're looking for easy, interesting vegetable-led dishes too; *The Green Roasting Tin* always comes top of the list when I ask about your most-used book in the series. The title of this book could easily have been 'Eat Your Greens: A joyful, exuberant celebration of veg, from kale to cucumbers'. (You can see why I'm not in charge of book titles.) Plant-led food is great for your health, for the planet and – speaking as a cook – there's such a fun, flavour-packed variety of dishes you can make with them. And, in the current climate, it's a lot cheaper to cook green – some of the recipes in this book first appeared in my £1-per-portion *Guardian* column, and you'll find the majority of the other recipes wallet-friendly too (just ignore any references to saffron, or whenever I decadently suggest jarred rather than tinned beans as a treat). As with *The Quick Roasting Tin*, your second-favourite book in the *Tin* series, most of the recipes in this book can be made in under 30 minutes, with an entire chapter of under-15-minute meals for maximum (fuel) efficiency – as Dalek-like as that sounds. Oven-based recipes in this book often maximise the use of the oven by cooking food on all shelves (like the black pepper, cardamom & ginger roasted squash with lime & coriander spiked bulgur on page 164), and you can pop other things into the oven to cook alongside most of the single-tin dishes, making the most of having the oven on – think jacket potatoes, sweet potatoes, trays of cherry tomatoes with olive oil and garlic or cubes of leftover bread for croutons. (Definitely add garlic to those. Maybe rosemary too.)

Just under half of the recipes in this book are plant-based, with a good proportion of the vegetarian recipes easily veganisable, and well over half of the recipes are gluten-free. To see at a glance which recipes are which, look out for the coloured labels at the top of each recipe. I have so many friends and readers – including the brilliant editor of this book (hi, Tamsin!) – who are coeliac or gluten intolerant, so it was important to me that the book had plenty of options for gluten-free dinner solutions, and notes to adapt as many recipes as possible with substitutions, if needed (like the crisp, bread-topped kimchi cobbler on page 178). The nicest thing about both the gluten-free and vegan recipes in this book is that readers who are neither will barely notice – I certainly didn't when writing and testing, which is saying a lot, coming from both a bread and cheese fiend.

QUICK COOK, QUICK CARB

Let me introduce the chapters to you. In the first section of this book you've got weeknight wins, kicking off with the 15-minute meal chapter: Quick Cook, Quick Carb. Here, you've got sauces that are ready in as long as it takes to cook your pasta or noodles, so all these recipes will get your dinner on the table in under 15 minutes (unless you seriously overboil your pasta). Peanut butter noodles with chilli, garlic & tenderstem (page 32) is on almost constant rotation at home, often made with added fried, cubed tofu, then the chilli added later to make it toddler-friendly. We also have my all-time favourite pasta dish, super simple tagliatelle with mushrooms, tomato & spinach (page 24) at least once every couple of weeks. If there's nothing in the fridge other than a head of broccoli, spaghetti with chilli, broccoli & walnut pesto (page 30) is such an easy weeknight win.

DINNER IN 30

If you've got ever so slightly more time, Dinner in 30 does just what it says on the tin, with a mix of quick stovetop dishes like the crisp sweetcorn fritters with avocado, halloumi & hot honey (page 46) or mapo-style tofu with mushrooms, chilli & spring onions (page 56). I also bring you a mac and cheese (page 58) that has been years in the making, where I've finally hit on my favourite sauce without needing to make a béchamel – it's a rich triple-cheese mixture of mascarpone, ricotta and cheddar (with broccoli and cauliflower to get you to your five-a-day).

DINNER TODAY, LUNCH TOMORROW

It might interest readers of this book that the Dinner Today, Lunch Tomorrow chapter will have to be adapted for the Dutch market, because in the Netherlands they don't have a leftovers-as-packed-lunch culture, and actually just generally don't do packed lunches – it's sandwiches or lunch out every day. The decadence! (Though I am, of course, secretly impressed.) But for those who have eaten the entire Pret range several times over and would quite like some home-cooked food now, please, this chapter is for you. On hot days, take last night's broccoli, date, pecan & chilli chopped salad (page 84) for lunch, which is even nicer the next day, or pack a baguette and peanut butter to make a bánh mì from last night's lemongrass, turmeric & tofu noodles (page 86) – the tofu goes into noodles on day one, then acts as a brilliant bánh mì filler on day two. As the weather turns, I bring you the best cauliflower soup with chilli almond butter (page 68) and a warming butternut squash laksa (page 76) – you'll be the envy of your office.

FAMILY DINNERS

It makes life so much easier if your family are all eating the same thing, so the Family Dinners chapter includes recipes that children might eat, but if they don't, they're nice enough that you'll happily tuck into your portion – and finish theirs too. The crispy baked ravioli lasagne with mushrooms & basil pesto (page 100) is frankly nice enough to serve to adult friends. And as any toddler parent knows, you can never have too many muffin recipes – the spelt, cheddar & courgette muffins (page 112) are perfect for snack boxes, as are the roasted broccoli, mushroom & courgette puffs (page 114), made with shop-bought puff pastry for ease. Alba advises fellow toddlers that she switches between loving the main meal recipes in this chapter to absolutely refusing them the following week (with a crushing chorus of 'no, no, NO!') but will then wolf down a portion of the same thing a month later, or indeed the same evening if she eats it from one of our plates instead of her own. The snack recipes are thankfully met with favour any day of the week (and from any container).

LIGHT SHARING PLATES

At the time of writing, it's pushing 30°C outside, and this chapter is where I turn when friends come round to sit in the shade for an outdoor lunch, while I secretly wonder if it's legit for us to all sit in the children's paddling pool, glasses of wine in hand. (When you see a paddling pool with an integrated bar and table on *Dragon's Den*, you'll know where they got their inspiration.) For a low-effort, celebratory sharing feast, I love serving the marinated butterbeans & tomatoes with pistachio & spring onion pesto (page 148) alongside the fennel with burrata, broad beans & pomegranate (page 132). Turmeric-fried aubergines with yogurt, chilli-butter cashew nuts & coriander (page 134) is another of my new all-time favourite dishes – and you can easily put several of these together within an hour. You can prep the food before your guests arrive, leaving you with nothing to do but pour drinks and enjoy the company.

BIG DISHES, BIG FLAVOURS

For colder nights, I've picked my favourite substantial dinners for Big Dishes, Big Flavours – think spiced roasted tomato & mushroom biryani pie with cucumber raita (page 174) or, another of my favourite new dishes that looks and tastes restaurant-fancy but is actually just a couple of roasting tins put together, miso barley mushrooms with coriander pesto (page 162). Given that the room I'm in currently feels like an oven and thinking about hot food is quite a tough job, I'll leave you to flick through this chapter on a day that's a little cooler.

BATCH COOK

Do you batch-cook? My sister inspired me to start, as she's the queen of Sunday afternoon cooking. I love the convenience of not having to cook on a Tuesday night because I was organised enough to make a one-tin pasta sauce with aubergines, tomatoes, capers & pine nuts (page 196) at the weekend. In this chapter, the coconut dal with roasted sweet potatoes & chilli-lime pickled onions (page 198) is a particular favourite, and I could eat the Spanish-style chickpeas with garlic & spinach (page 200) on a weekly basis. My infant daughter, despite having a whole chapter to herself, loves the slow-cooked rosemary & red wine mushroom ragu (page 194), and although you almost certainly have a favourite bean chilli recipe up your sleeve, you have to try my latest version, the ultimate bean chilli with walnuts & chocolate (page 202).

The recipes in this book have certainly helped me cook through the first year of our growing family, and I hope there are many that you will turn to again and again to get easy, low-hassle, flavour-packed weeknight meals on the table.

INGREDIENTS, A NOTE

As ever, you can find what you need for the vast majority of these recipes in your local supermarket, because you may not always have the energy for specialist things. The two exceptions to this are really so good that I promise it's worth the extra effort – if you can find jarred beans or chickpeas rather than tinned, they are a luxurious addition to a largely vegetarian or vegan diet. The flavour and texture really are incomparable – I love buying them as a treat for dishes where the beans won't cook for more than 10 minutes or so. (Tinned beans are much better for slow-cooked dishes.) You can find jarred beans in Waitrose, online on Ocado, in local delis or even on Amazon. That said, the recipes in this book will improve ordinary tinned beans no end – but if you can get hold of a jar, it's worth it.

The second exception is vegan cheese. I tried quite a lot of it during the eight months that I attempted to go vegan and am happy to report that the best I found bears no comparison to commercial offerings. It is made by a company called Palace Culture from fermented cashew nuts, and it would happily sit among the best dairy cheeses in terms of flavour and texture. You can order online, and my favourites include the kimchi cheese, in a blind test you'd be hard pressed to tell the difference from dairy. My husband, who isn't vegan by any stretch, loves them on an alternative cheeseboard, as do I – use them in any recipe in this book that calls for a soft cheese. For a hard cheese to go on pasta, try the easy vegan parmesan recipe (page 230).

All the dishes in this book are seasoned with Maldon sea salt, because it's my favourite. If you use level teaspoons of other kinds of sea salt (particularly fine sea salt), your dishes will be much saltier. Do bear this in mind and season with caution. Finally, I don't always specify what type of butter or yogurt to use (salted, unsalted, plain, Greek, etc.) because you know what you tend to buy in, and the recipes will be just fine with either.

QUICK COOK, QUICK CARB

If it takes 12 minutes to boil your pasta, it'll take 12 minutes or less to cook these sauces while your pasta (or polenta) boils. And even less time to stir-fry your ingredients for the noodle dishes. You'll note a distinct preference for linguine, spaghetti and tagliatelle here, because they're my favourite types of pasta, but you can of course use other pasta shapes as you wish.

QUICK COOK, QUICK CARB

SUPER SIMPLE TAGLIATELLE WITH MUSHROOMS, TOMATO & SPINACH (VEGANISABLE)

MISO BUTTER NOODLES WITH TOMATOES & SPRING ONIONS

GREEN LINGUINE WITH KALE, WHITE BEANS & FETA

SPAGHETTI WITH CHILLI, BROCCOLI & WALNUT PESTO

PEANUT BUTTER NOODLES WITH CHILLI, GARLIC & TENDERSTEM (VG)

CHERRY TOMATO, CANNELLINI BEAN & RICOTTA PASTA

BLACK BEAN NOODLES WITH MUSHROOMS & PAK CHOI (VG)

LINGUINE WITH COURGETTES, PINE NUTS & CHILLI (VEGANISABLE)

GRIDDLED ASPARAGUS, BLACK OLIVE & LEMON POLENTA WITH FETA (GF)

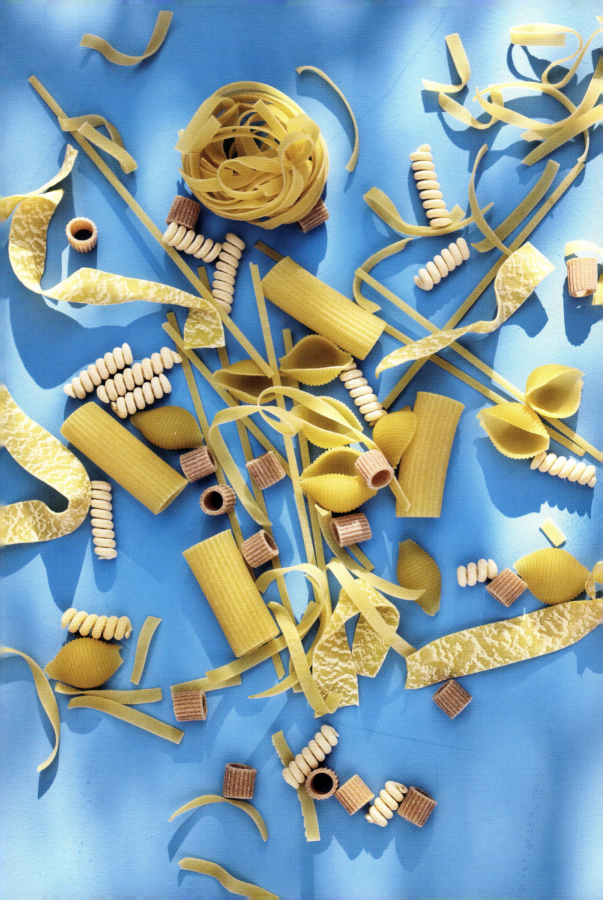

SUPER SIMPLE TAGLIATELLE WITH MUSHROOMS, TOMATO & SPINACH

Serves: 2   Prep: 15 minutes   Cook: 12 minutes

This is a dish I first had on holiday in Mallorca after wandering into a bar for a glass of very cold white wine and asking if they did food. 'We don't really,' said the waitress, 'but I can make you something.' What appeared was this: a ridiculously good dish of tagliatelle with garlic mushrooms, cherry tomatoes, cream and wilted spinach. Finished with a squeeze of lemon, it's been a go-to dinner at home ever since, and it's certain to become part of your repertoire too.

80–100g tagliatelle per person

2 tablespoons olive oil, plus extra as needed

2 cloves garlic, finely grated

250g chestnut mushrooms, sliced

200g cherry tomatoes, halved

150g spinach

100ml double cream

½ lemon, juice only, plus extra as needed

Sea salt flakes and freshly ground black pepper

Vegetarian parmesan, grated, to serve

VEGANISE: Replace the double cream with vegan cream or cream cheese, or you can leave it out altogether – it's a delicious sauce either way. Top with vegan parmesan (page 230).

Make sure you've got all your vegetables chopped before you start, then bring a large saucepan of salted water to the boil. Cook the tagliatelle according to the packet instructions, or until cooked to your liking (10 minutes works for me).

Meanwhile, heat the oil in a large frying pan over a medium to high heat, then add the garlic and mushrooms with a pinch of salt. Stir-fry for 5 minutes, then add the cherry tomatoes. Cook gently for 2–3 minutes – you're aiming for them to soften rather than completely break down – then add the spinach and let it wilt. Add the double cream, a teaspoon more salt and a good grind of black pepper and stir. Let it bubble for a minute, then turn off the heat.

Your tagliatelle should now be ready; drain it, reserving a mugful of the cooking water, then return the tagliatelle to the pan and add the mushroom and tomato sauce. Gently stir to coat the pasta in the sauce, adding a little pasta water and a splash of olive oil if needed to loosen the mix. Add the lemon juice, then taste and adjust the salt as needed, with a squeeze more lemon if you wish.

Serve in warmed bowls with more freshly ground black pepper and parmesan.

MISO BUTTER NOODLES WITH TOMATOES & SPRING ONIONS

Serves: 2   Prep: 10 minutes   Cook: 10 minutes

This ridiculously lovely noodle dish takes just minutes to put together and is by far my favourite emergency dinner (I almost always have cherry tomatoes on the side and miso and spring onions in the fridge). Having tried this dish variously with every type of noodle, I can confirm the best are bouncy, thick udon noodles. If you haven't got pine nuts in, chopped salted peanuts are a great alternative topping.

2 handfuls pine nuts
30g salted butter
2 cloves garlic, finely grated
2 inches ginger, finely grated
250g good cherry tomatoes, halved
4 spring onions, thickly sliced
30g good white miso paste
1 tablespoon rice vinegar
200g straight-to-wok thick udon noodles
Sea salt flakes, to taste

Toast your pine nuts in whichever way works best for you – a small frying pan over a low to medium heat with razor-sharp attention usually does the trick; just be sure to shake the pan or stir frequently.

Meanwhile, heat the butter in a large frying pan; when foaming, add the garlic and ginger over a medium heat. Stir-fry for 30 seconds, then add the tomatoes and spring onions. Stir-fry over a medium to low heat for 5 minutes, then gently stir through the miso and rice vinegar.

Stir the straight-to-wok noodles through the hot miso tomato butter, stir-fry for 2 minutes to soften the noodles, then taste and add salt as needed (you shouldn't need much as the miso is already salty). Serve hot, scattered with the toasted pine nuts.

NOTE: If you're not a fan of straight-to-wok noodles, just use your favourite brand of udon noodles and cook them according to the packet instructions.

GREEN LINGUINE WITH KALE, WHITE BEANS & FETA

Serves: 2   Prep: 5 minutes   Cook: 15 minutes

This is an excellent way to update your classic pesto pasta, with sharp feta and lemon alongside the fresh basil pesto and cream cheese sauce. Haricot beans and kale add texture, and they're great for you – a winning dish all around.

Handful blanched hazelnuts
180–200g linguine
150g kale, thinly sliced
1 x 400g tin haricot beans, drained and rinsed
1 pot chilled fresh basil pesto (approx. 140g)
100g cream cheese
1 lemon, juice only, plus extra as needed
100g feta cheese, crumbled
Sea salt flakes, to taste

Toast the hazelnuts for 10 minutes in a preheated oven at 180°C fan/200°C/gas 6, or for 5 minutes in a small frying pan, shaking frequently.

Bring your largest saucepan of salted water to the boil, then add the linguine and cook for 10–12 minutes, or until done to your liking. Add the sliced kale after 9 minutes, and the haricot beans just before you drain the pasta, so they can warm through.

Drain the pasta, beans and kale, reserving a good mugful of the cooking water. Add the pesto and cream cheese to the pan along with the lemon juice and mix well, adding the reserved pasta water by the tablespoon as needed to create a smooth sauce. Taste and adjust the salt and lemon juice as needed and serve immediately in warmed bowls, topped with the crumbled feta and toasted hazelnuts.

NOTE: If you don't have hazelnuts, walnuts would work really well here too.

SPAGHETTI WITH CHILLI, BROCCOLI & WALNUT PESTO

Serves: 4   Prep: 10 minutes   Cook: 12 minutes

This has to be one of my favourite ways to make pesto – broccoli is the perfect base alongside chilli and walnuts. I've given quantities to serve four below, because even a small head of broccoli makes a lot of pesto, but if you're cooking for one or two, I'd suggest just reducing the amount of pasta, and stashing the remaining pesto in the fridge for up to 2 days, or in the freezer in portions for future emergencies.

350g spaghetti
50g walnuts
1 small head broccoli,
   cut into florets
1 clove garlic
50g parmesan
150ml olive oil/extra virgin
   olive oil
1 lemon, juice only
½–1 teaspoon chilli flakes
1 teaspoon sea salt flakes,
   or to taste

To serve
30g walnuts, roughly chopped
Parmesan
Freshly ground black pepper

Bring a large saucepan of salted water to the boil and cook the spaghetti until al dente (about 10 minutes), or until cooked to your liking.

Toast 30g walnuts for the topping in a small, dry frying pan while you get on with the pesto – this should take 4–5 minutes over a medium heat, shaking the pan frequently.

Tip 50g untoasted walnuts, the broccoli, garlic and 50g cheese into a food processor and pulse until you have a thick, rough, green rubble. Add the olive oil, lemon juice, chilli flakes and sea salt and blitz again briefly to combine. Set aside.

Once the pasta is done, drain well, reserving a mugful of the pasta water. Return the spaghetti to the pan and gently stir through the broccoli pesto, adding the pasta water a tablespoon at a time to loosen as needed. Taste and adjust the salt, then serve immediately, topped with more parmesan, freshly ground black pepper, the toasted walnuts and the fresh basil leaves.

PEANUT BUTTER NOODLES WITH CHILLI, GARLIC & TENDERSTEM

Serves: 2   Prep: 10 minutes   Cook: 8–10 minutes

This is my most-requested noodle dish at home (ranging from the two-year-old to the thirty-something-year-old. No doubt the dog would chime in, too, if she were allowed noodles). If you grab a packet of broccoli on your way home, the rest of this recipe is all storecupboard ingredients, and can be on the table within minutes. It's best served immediately, as the sauce will thicken dramatically the longer it sits around.

250g noodles of your choice

2 tablespoons sesame oil, plus extra to finish

2 cloves garlic, finely grated

1 red chilli, finely chopped

250g tenderstem broccoli, fairly finely chopped

3 tablespoons soy sauce, plus extra as needed

25ml rice vinegar or juice of 2 limes, plus extra as needed

50g smooth peanut butter

200ml water

Put the noodles in a heatproof bowl, cover with just-boiled water and set aside for 5 minutes, or cook according to the packet instructions – rinse under cold water if needed.

Heat the oil in a wok or large, deep frying pan over a medium heat and add the garlic and chilli. Stir-fry for 30 seconds, then add the broccoli and stir-fry for 5 minutes. Add the soy sauce, rice vinegar or lime juice, peanut butter and half the water, and stir until the peanut butter is smooth and amalgamated, about the consistency of double cream (add more water if you need to). Add the drained noodles and gently stir them through the sauce, adding the remaining water to loosen the mix as needed.

It's now imperative (as bossy as that sounds) that you taste and adjust the soy sauce and vinegar or lime juice as needed, because the water will have somewhat diluted the flavour, and you'll have needed more or less water depending on your brand of peanut butter. Once it tastes just right to you, serve immediately in your favourite bowls. Drizzle with a little sesame oil to finish.

NOTE: For extra protein, add cubed smoked tofu when you stir-fry the broccoli.

CHERRY TOMATO, CANNELLINI BEAN & RICOTTA PASTA

Serves: 2   Prep: 10 minutes   Cook: 12–15 minutes

This is one of those 'you barely need a recipe' recipes, and yet I include it because there's something so lovely about a fresh cherry tomato sauce with cannellini beans for added protein and texture. I like to top the sauce with a spoonful of ricotta – for a vegan version, I highly recommend the Palace Culture vegan ricotta (or feta) as an alternative (see page 17).

180–200g wholewheat
  or ordinary fusilli
2 tablespoons olive oil
2 cloves garlic, finely grated
350g good cherry tomatoes,
  quartered
1 x 400g tin cannellini beans,
  drained and rinsed
Handful basil leaves, roughly
  torn or chopped
½ lemon, zest and juice
Good glug extra virgin olive oil
125g ricotta
Sea salt flakes and freshly
  ground black pepper

Bring a large saucepan of salted water to the boil and cook the fusilli according to the packet instructions, or for 12–15 minutes until al dente – (I love wholewheat fusilli but find it takes a long time to cook).

Meanwhile, heat the olive oil in a large saucepan over a medium heat and add the garlic and cherry tomatoes. Soften for 3–4 minutes before adding the cannellini beans and most of the basil leaves. Simmer over a low heat, stirring occasionally, until the cherry tomatoes have broken down and the pasta is ready.

Drain the pasta, reserving a mugful of the cooking water, and stir the pasta through the tomato and cannellini bean sauce. Add the lemon zest and juice, a good glug of extra virgin olive oil and a little of the pasta water, if needed, to create a nice smooth sauce. Taste and season with salt as needed.

Divide the pasta between two warmed bowls, then top with the ricotta, freshly ground pepper and remaining basil leaves, and serve hot.

BLACK BEAN NOODLES WITH MUSHROOMS & PAK CHOI

Serves: 2   Prep: 10 minutes   Cook: 10 minutes

Good black bean sauce – the thick, concentrated kind in a jar, rather than in a bottle – is an instant flavour hit in the kitchen. It packs a real punch – just use it a teaspoon at a time if you've got the good stuff. Paired with mushrooms, pak choi and noodles, it's a filling weeknight win. Add cubed tofu for protein, if you wish.

2 tablespoons sesame oil, plus extra for drizzling

2 inches ginger, finely grated

2 cloves garlic, finely grated

250g chestnut mushrooms, thinly sliced

2 large pak choi, thickly sliced

3 teaspoons black bean sauce (I used Lee Kum Kee black bean garlic sauce), plus extra as needed

2 portions straight-to-wok thick udon noodles

Lime wedges, to serve

Handful salted peanuts, to serve

Heat the oil in a large wok or deep frying pan over a high heat and add the ginger and garlic. Let them sizzle for 30 seconds, then add the mushrooms and stir-fry for 5 minutes until well browned and the liquid has evaporated. Add the pak choi and stir-fry for a further 2 minutes until starting to wilt.

Add the black bean sauce and the straight-to-wok noodles. Stir-fry for a further 2 minutes until everything is glossily coated in the sauce, adding a dash more sesame oil and a few tablespoons of hot water as needed, to loosen the sauce. Taste the noodles and add a little more black bean sauce, as required.

Serve with the lime wedges to squeeze over and a handful of salted peanuts for crunch.

LINGUINE WITH COURGETTES, PINE NUTS & CHILLI

Serves: 2   Prep: 10 minutes   Cook: 15 minutes

This is one of my favourite courgette dishes, and it takes just minutes to put together. The grated courgettes turn into a silky sauce for the pasta, spiked with chilli and pine nuts for interest. It's easy enough to make on a weeknight, but smart enough to serve to friends. As it's such a simple dish, the secret is to keep tasting and adjusting the salt and lemon until it's just right for you.

200g linguine

2 large or 3 medium courgettes, grated

1 tablespoon butter

1 tablespoon olive oil

2 cloves garlic, finely grated

½–1 teaspoon chilli flakes

50g pine nuts

40g vegetarian parmesan, grated

½ lemon, juice only, plus extra as needed

Sea salt flakes, to taste

VEGANISE: Substitute the butter with oil, and use vegan parmesan (page 230).

Bring a large saucepan of salted water to the boil and cook the linguine according to the packet instructions, to your preferred level of al dente (I like 12 minutes).

Meanwhile, tip the grated courgettes into a clean tea towel and squeeze over a bowl to remove as much liquid as possible. Heat the butter in a large frying pan; when foaming, add the oil, garlic and chilli. Stir-fry for 30 seconds, then add the grated courgette and a big pinch of sea salt.

Turn the heat down to medium and cook the courgette for 5–6 minutes, stirring occasionally. Meanwhile, toast the pine nuts over a medium to low heat in a small, dry frying pan until there's a good colour on them, watching them like a hawk so they don't burn. This should take 4–5 minutes.

Drain the linguine, retaining a mugful of cooking water, then return the pasta to the pan. Add the cooked courgettes, 30g of the parmesan, the lemon juice, a big pinch of sea salt and stir well, adding a little pasta water as needed until you have a silky consistency. Taste and adjust the salt and add more lemon juice if needed. (The difference between this dish being amazing or ordinary is in this last step, so keep tasting!) Serve hot, scattered with the pine nuts.

GRIDDLED ASPARAGUS, BLACK OLIVE & LEMON POLENTA WITH FETA

Serves: 4   Prep: 15 minutes   Cook: 10–12 minutes

This is a lovely bowl of comfort food – the sort of dish you want to take to the sofa to eat with a big spoon. It's perfect for a colder spring evening when asparagus is in season. At other times of the year, use tenderstem broccoli instead – just blanch in boiling water for 2 minutes before griddling. If you have a bottle of good chilli oil, you could drizzle that over instead of extra virgin olive oil to finish.

200g asparagus tips
1 tablespoon olive oil
700ml boiling vegetable stock
  (gluten-free, if required)
150g quick-cook polenta
  (not the precooked block!)
150g pitted black olives,
  roughly chopped
250g ricotta
1 lemon, zest and juice
200g feta, crumbled
Handful toasted flaked
  almonds
Sea salt flakes and freshly
  ground black pepper
Extra virgin olive oil, to serve

Preheat a griddle pan over a high heat. Toss the asparagus with the oil, then griddle for 2 minutes on each side (you may need to do this in batches depending on the size of your pan). Transfer to a plate and scatter with sea salt flakes.

Meanwhile, bring the stock to the boil in a large saucepan. Add the polenta and stir for 4 minutes until thickened. Add the olives, ricotta and lemon zest and juice, then taste and season with salt as needed.

Divide the polenta between four warmed bowls, then top with the asparagus, a drizzle of extra virgin olive oil, the crumbled feta, flaked almonds and plenty of freshly ground black pepper. Serve hot.

NOTE: This dish serves four, but I'd make the full quantity of polenta even if you're cooking for two – you can spread out the leftover cooked polenta on a buttered baking tray, then follow the recipe on page 108 to make crisp polenta bites the next day.

DINNER IN 30

These recipes take 10 minutes to prep
and 30 minutes tops to cook, with plenty
of hands-free, one-pot and one-tin options.
If there isn't a carb included in the recipe, just
turn to page 232 for quick-cook rice options.

2

DINNER IN 30

CRISP SWEETCORN FRITTERS
WITH AVOCADO, HALLOUMI & HOT HONEY

ALL-IN-ONE ORZO WITH BAKED FETA,
TOMATOES & OLIVES

EASY PANEER CURRY
WITH SPINACH, CREAM & LEMON (GF)

ROASTED TOFU & AUBERGINE
WITH CHILLI-PEANUT SATAY SAUCE (VG, GF)

PEA, TARRAGON
& CREAM CHEESE TART (CAN BE GF)

MAPO-STYLE TOFU WITH MUSHROOMS,
CHILLI & SPRING ONIONS (VG)

20-MINUTE CRISP-TOPPED BROCCOLI
& CAULIFLOWER MAC & CHEESE

CHICKPEA, CAULIFLOWER
& COCONUT CURRY (VG, GF)

PARMESAN & LEMON TENDERSTEM
WITH GREEN PEA ORZOTTO (VEGANISABLE)

CRISP SWEETCORN FRITTERS WITH AVOCADO, HALLOUMI & HOT HONEY

Serves: 2 adults and 2 children   Prep: 10 minutes   Cook: 25 minutes

I enjoy the brunch-for-dinner vibes of this dish, and it's easy enough to make on a weeknight after work. If you keep the hot honey for yourself, it's a winner with children too. My top timesaving tips: slice up the avocado and halloumi while you fry the fritters and use a second pan to cook the halloumi slices. It's a delicious enough dinner that your resident washing-up volunteer (!) won't mind the additional pan.

300g frozen sweetcorn, defrosted (or the equivalent drained from tins)
150g self-raising flour
1 teaspoon baking powder
1 teaspoon smoked paprika
1 teaspoon sea salt flakes
2 nice free-range eggs
100ml milk
2 avocados, sliced
1 lime, juice only
Olive oil, for frying
225–250g halloumi, cut into ½cm slices
6 tablespoons honey
1 teaspoon chipotle chilli flakes
Greek yogurt, to serve

Mix the sweetcorn, flour, baking powder, smoked paprika and salt together in a bowl. In a small jug, whisk the eggs and milk together, then stir this into the sweetcorn mixture to form a thick batter. Dress the sliced avocado with the lime juice.

Preheat the oven to 50°C fan/70°C/gas ¼. Heat ½ tablespoon of oil in a large, heavy-based frying pan over a medium heat. Drop heaped tablespoons of the batter (you want about 1 ½ tablespoons of batter per fritter) into the pan, reasonably well spaced apart, and fry for 2 minutes on each side, adjusting the temperature as needed so they don't cook too quickly. Remove to a shallow roasting tin lined with kitchen paper, then transfer the tin to the warming oven while you continue with the rest of the batter, using ½ tablespoon of oil per batch.

For speed, use a second dry pan or griddle pan to fry the halloumi slices over a medium heat for 1 ½–2 minutes on each side until golden brown.

Once you're finished frying the fritters, add the honey to the pan with the chipotle flakes and heat on low for 1 minute until bubbling. Serve the fritters with the halloumi, avocado and yogurt alongside, and drizzle over the hot honey just before serving.

ALL-IN-ONE ORZO WITH BAKED FETA, TOMATOES & OLIVES

Serves: 2 generously   Prep: 10 minutes   Cook: 25 minutes

This is an update on one of my favourite *Green Roasting Tin* recipes, a really simple dish of baked orzo with fresh cherry tomatoes. Here, I add in a big square of feta to bake on top of the pasta, along with olives for a briny hit of flavour – all your food groups in one go. It's perfect for a light dinner on a summer evening.

200g orzo
450ml boiling vegetable stock
300g baby plum or cherry
    tomatoes, halved
50g olives, pitted and halved
200g feta cheese
2 tablespoons olive oil
Couple of handfuls fresh basil
    leaves
Freshly ground black pepper

To serve
Extra virgin olive oil
Chilli flakes (optional)

Preheat the oven to 180°C fan/200°C/gas 6.

Put the orzo into a medium roasting tin, pour over the boiling stock and stir, then top with the tomatoes and olives.

Place the block of feta cheese in the middle of the dish, then drizzle over the olive oil, a scatter of fresh basil leaves (reserve some for later) and a good grind of freshly ground black pepper. Transfer to the oven to bake for 25 minutes.

Carefully remove the baked feta with a fish slice and give the orzo a good mix with a wooden spoon before serving, then replace the feta as pictured. Scatter over the reserved basil leaves and top with a drizzle of extra virgin olive oil and a scatter of chilli flakes. Once cooked, let the dish stand for a few minutes before serving hot.

EASY PANEER CURRY WITH SPINACH, CREAM & LEMON

Serves: 4   Prep: 15 minutes   Cook: 20 minutes

This is my version of palak paneer, one of my favourite curries – you can put it together in almost half an hour from start to finish. Blitzing the spinach, spices and cream together into a sauce really brings the flavours together, but if you haven't got a high-speed blender or food processor, just give the spinach a bit of a chop before cooking it.

400g paneer,
  cut into 1cm cubes
3 tablespoons neutral
  or olive oil
1 teaspoon cumin seeds
1 onion, finely chopped
½ teaspoon ground turmeric
1 teaspoon ground coriander
1 teaspoon fennel seeds
1 teaspoon ground ginger
½ teaspoon chilli flakes
200g spinach
150ml single cream
1 teaspoon sea salt flakes, plus
  extra as needed
½ lemon, juice only
Basmati rice (page 232), naan
  or flatbreads (gluten-free,
  if required), to serve

NOTE: My mum likes to drizzle a little extra cream over curries like this before serving, as shown opposite.

Put the cubed paneer into a large heatproof bowl, cover with just-boiled water and set aside for 10 minutes. Drain the paneer well and pat it dry with a tea towel. Meanwhile, heat 2 tablespoons of the oil in a large, non-stick frying pan over a low heat and add the cumin seeds. Let them sizzle for 30 seconds, then add the onion and stir-fry over a medium heat for 10 minutes, stirring frequently until golden brown.

Add the remaining spices and chilli flakes to the pan with the onions and stir-fry for 30 seconds over a low heat before adding the spinach. Cover and let the spinach cook for a couple of minutes before removing the lid and giving it a stir to completely wilt. Transfer the spinach and onions to a high-speed blender and set aside to cool.

Heat the remaining tablespoon of oil in the frying pan and add the paneer. Fry over a medium heat for 2–3 minutes on each side until golden brown. Meanwhile, blitz the cooled spinach with the cream and sea salt. Once the paneer is golden brown all over, add the spinach sauce back into the pan, stir and simmer for a further 2–3 minutes. Turn off the heat and add the lemon juice and a splash of just-boiled water to thin the sauce, then taste and adjust the salt as needed. Serve hot, with rice, naan or flatbreads alongside.

ROASTED TOFU & AUBERGINE WITH CHILLI-PEANUT SATAY SAUCE

Serves: 2   Prep: 15 minutes   Cook: 30 minutes

If you're a fan of quick, plant-based roasting-tin dinners, this is certain to become a go-to in your house, as it is in mine – if my husband spots a block of smoked tofu in the fridge, he'll most likely ask if we're having this for dinner. The chilli-peanut sauce is what makes this addictive, with freshness from just-torn mint and crunch from salted peanuts at the end – just serve on a pile of fluffy white rice, or noodles if you wish.

225g smoked tofu,
  cut into 1 ½cm chunks
1 large aubergine,
  cut into 2cm chunks
2 cloves garlic, finely grated
2 tablespoons sesame oil
2 tablespoons soy sauce
  (or tamari if gluten-free)

For the dressing
60g peanut butter
  (smooth or crunchy)
1 tablespoon sesame oil
2 tablespoons soy sauce
  (or tamari if gluten-free),
  plus extra as needed
2 tablespoons water,
  plus extra as needed
1 red chilli, finely chopped
1–2 limes, zest and juice

To serve
Basmati rice (page 232)
  or noodles (gluten-free,
  if required)
Handful fresh mint leaves,
  roughly chopped
Finely chopped red chilli
Handful salted peanuts

Preheat the oven to 180°C fan/200°C/gas 6.

Squeeze the excess water from the tofu with kitchen paper or a clean tea towel, then tip the aubergine and tofu into a roasting tin large enough to hold everything in one layer. Mix through the garlic, sesame oil and soy sauce. Transfer to the oven to roast for 30 minutes until the aubergine is cooked through and the tofu is starting to crisp.

While that cooks, mix together the peanut butter, sesame oil, soy sauce, water, chilli and the zest and juice of 1 lime for the dressing. Depending on the brand of peanut butter, you may need to add more water, a tablespoon at a time, to get a sauce the consistency of thick cream. Once you're happy with the consistency, taste again and add more soy sauce and lime juice if you need it.

Scatter the tofu and aubergine over the hot rice or noodles, pour over the dressing, and top with the mint leaves, chopped red chilli and salted peanuts.

NOTE: If you like a slightly sweet satay sauce, add 1 tablespoon agave or brown/palm sugar to the dressing.

PEA, TARRAGON & CREAM CHEESE TART

Serves: 4   Prep: 10 minutes   Cook: 30 minutes

This simple puff pastry tart is nice enough to make when friends come over, but easy enough that you could make it for a quick weeknight dinner. Just unroll your puff pastry, top with a mixture of quickly cooked frozen peas, eggs and crème fraîche, scatter over your cheese and voilà! An easy quiche-adjacent meal. I love the background complexity from adding fresh tarragon, but if you don't have it or aren't keen on the flavour, just let the Boursin cheese do the herb heavy-lifting for the dish.

250g frozen peas, defrosted
2 sprigs tarragon, leaves
  finely chopped
4 nice free-range eggs
100g full-fat crème fraîche
1 lemon, zest and juice
½ teaspoon sea salt flakes,
  plus extra to serve
150g Boursin garlic and herb
  cheese (or similar)
1 x 320g sheet all butter
  (if available) ready-rolled
  puff pastry

Preheat the oven to 180°C fan/200°C/gas 6.

Boil the peas in a saucepan of water for 2 minutes, then drain and rinse well under cold water.

Meanwhile, whisk the tarragon, eggs, crème fraîche and lemon zest together with the sea salt, then stir through the peas.

Unroll the puff pastry into a 20cm by 30cm roasting tin, just small enough that the pastry comes up the sides to form a lip. Pour in the pea and crème fraîche mixture, dot the Boursin cheese over evenly, then bake for 25 minutes until the pastry is crisp and golden brown.

Scatter over a pinch of sea salt flakes and finish with a squeeze of lemon juice before serving hot or at room temperature.

NOTE: If you have bought a packet of tarragon just for this dish, strip the leaves into a small freezer bag and freeze for future use.

MAKE IT GF: Use gluten-free ready-rolled puff pastry.

MAPO-STYLE TOFU WITH MUSHROOMS, CHILLI & SPRING ONIONS

Serves: 2   Prep: 15 minutes   Cook: 15 minutes

My recipe for mapo tofu takes great liberties with Fuchsia Dunlop's wonderful recipe in *Every Grain of Rice* – I replace the meat with mushrooms and the wobbly tofu for firm, only because I prefer the texture. It's perfect with a big bowl of fluffy white rice. Don't panic if you can't find Sichuan chilli bean paste easily, I've successfully (if unorthodoxly) used Lee Kum Kee's chilli garlic sauce, which incorporates fermented soy beans. Once you have either sauce in, you'll be making this on a regular rotation – it's addictively good.

225g firm smoked
   or unsmoked tofu,
   cut into 1 ½cm cubes
2 tablespoons sesame oil
250g chestnut mushrooms,
   finely chopped
4 spring onions, thinly sliced
   (white and green
   parts separated)
1 inch ginger, finely grated
2 cloves garlic, finely grated
2 ½ tablespoons Sichuan
   chilli bean paste
   (or, in a pinch, another
   chilli paste-like sauce)
1 tablespoon black bean sauce
   (or 1 tablespoon fermented
   black beans, if you have them)
100ml water
½ teaspoon Sichuan
   peppercorns, ground
   in a pestle and mortar (optional)
Sea salt flakes, to taste
Basmati rice (page 232),
   to serve

Soak the tofu in a heatproof bowl of just-boiled water and set aside for 10 minutes.

Meanwhile, heat the sesame oil in a large frying pan or wok over a medium to high heat and add the mushrooms, the white part of the spring onions, the ginger and garlic. Stir-fry for 10 minutes until the moisture has evaporated from the mushrooms. Drain the tofu and pat dry with kitchen paper.

Add the chilli bean paste and black bean sauce (or their substitutions) to the pan and stir-fry for 30 seconds before adding the water. Stir through, then add the drained tofu and gently stir to mix. Bring to the boil, then gently simmer for 2–3 minutes, adding the remaining sliced spring onion greens for the last 2 minutes. Taste and adjust the salt as needed.

Scatter over the ground Sichuan peppercorns (if using), and serve hot with fluffy white rice.

MAKE IT GF: Check the labels on your shop-bought sauces/pastes.

20-MINUTE CRISP-TOPPED BROCCOLI & CAULIFLOWER MAC & CHEESE

Serves: 2 adults and 2 children   Prep: 10 minutes   Cook: 20 minutes

This rich, indulgent mascarpone and ricotta-based mac and cheese might be one of my proudest creations. I rarely want to stand stirring béchamel sauce on a weeknight, so I've experimented variously with crème fraîche (quite good, made it into an earlier book) and crème fraîche and egg (less good) before hitting the holy grail – mascarpone, ricotta and cheddar. Stirred into hot pasta and just-blanched cauliflower and broccoli with a generous amount of Dijon mustard, it's a crowd-pleasing weeknight win.

250g macaroni (or pasta shape of your choice)
1 x 250g tub ricotta
1 x 250g tub mascarpone
100g mature cheddar, grated
3 heaped tablespoons smooth Dijon mustard (not optional! It emulsifies the sauce)
1 teaspoon sea salt flakes (optional)
1 small head cauliflower, cut into medium florets
250g tenderstem broccoli, roughly chopped (or 1 small head broccoli, cut into medium florets)

For the topping
80g mature cheddar, grated
40g panko or white breadcrumbs
Olive oil
Freshly ground black pepper

Bring a really large saucepan of salted water to the boil (use your largest, as you need to stir everything in it later). Cook the macaroni for 9–10 minutes or until done to your liking.

Mix the ricotta, mascarpone, grated cheese, Dijon mustard and salt, if using, in a large bowl.

Add the cauliflower and broccoli to the pan with the pasta and cook for the last 2 minutes until the pasta is just cooked and vegetables are blanched. Drain well, then return the pasta and vegetables to the pan. Stir through the mascarpone sauce until everything is well coated. Taste and add salt as needed.

Preheat the grill to medium-high (mine says 200°C). Spread out the pasta and veg in a large, shallow roasting tin (it'll give you maximum surface area for crunch). Scatter over the mature cheddar and then the breadcrumbs, then finish with a drizzle of olive oil and a good grind of black pepper. Pop the tray under the grill for 3–4 minutes, keeping an eye on it; if needed, rotate the pan before grilling for a further 2–3 minutes until evenly golden brown and crisp – it's worth staying by the grill to catch it at the right moment. Serve hot.

CHICKPEA, CAULIFLOWER & COCONUT CURRY

Serves: 4   Prep: 15 minutes   Cook: 30 minutes

I could eat a different chickpea curry every week, which is why you'll find at least three in this book. This version, with cauliflower, coconut milk and lime, is packed with flavour – just rereading the recipe now makes me hungry. It's also wallet-friendly, as it first appeared in my £1-per-portion column in the *Guardian*. Do make the full portion even if you're serving two, as leftovers are even nicer the next day.

2 tablespoons neutral
   or olive oil
1 teaspoon cumin seeds
1 onion, finely chopped
2 inches ginger, finely grated
2 cloves garlic, finely grated
1 heaped teaspoon ground
   cumin
1 heaped teaspoon ground
   coriander
½ teaspoon ground turmeric
1 teaspoon chilli flakes
1 teaspoon sea salt flakes,
   plus extra as needed
1 x 400g tin coconut milk
1 small cauliflower,
   cut into small florets
1 x 400g tin chickpeas,
   drained and rinsed
150g spinach
2 limes, juice only
Flatbreads (gluten-free,
   if required), or basmati rice
   (page 232), to serve

Heat the oil in a large saucepan over a medium heat and add the cumin seeds. Fry for 30 seconds, then add the onion and cook over a medium to low heat for 10 minutes, stirring occasionally, until golden brown.

Add the ginger, garlic, cumin, coriander, turmeric, chilli flakes and sea salt and stir-fry for 2 minutes over a low heat. Add the coconut milk, stir if not smooth, then add the cauliflower and chickpeas. Bring to the boil, then simmer for 10–15 minutes or until the cauliflower is just cooked through. Add the spinach and cook for a further 2 minutes or until wilted.

Let the curry stand for 10 minutes to allow the flavours to mingle, then add the lime juice and taste and adjust the salt as needed. (The sauce will taste saltier than the chickpeas or cauliflower, so try a bit of everything together.) Serve hot, with flatbreads or rice on the side.

NOTE: If you have the oven on anyway, this is lovely with roasted cauliflower too. Just add it to the pan when you have 5 minutes left on the sauce.

PARMESAN & LEMON TENDERSTEM WITH GREEN PEA ORZOTTO

Serves: 2   Prep: 10 minutes   Cook: 25 minutes

I never get tired of cooking with orzo – in this elegant dinner for two, the pasta cooks on one shelf of the oven and you get a lovely char on the broccoli by roasting it on another. The lemon zest and juice in the dressing add a wonderful citrussy hit, rounded out by the parmesan. You can scatter over toasted hazelnuts to finish, if you wish.

200g orzo
200g frozen peas
400ml boiling vegetable stock
200g tenderstem broccoli
1 tablespoon olive oil
Handful hazelnuts, to serve
1 lemon, zest and juice
2 tablespoons extra virgin olive oil
30g vegetarian or vegan
  (page 230) parmesan, grated
Sea salt and freshly
  ground black pepper

Preheat the oven to 180°C fan. (You do need to use a fan oven, as you're cooking the orzo and tenderstem at the same time.) Put the orzo and frozen peas into a medium roasting tin, pour over the boiling stock, then transfer to the oven to bake for 25 minutes or until the orzo is cooked through.

Meanwhile, place the broccoli in a heatproof bowl and cover with just-boiled water. Leave to blanch for 2 minutes, then drain well. Transfer to a shallow roasting tin or baking tray, dress with the olive oil and ½ teaspoon of sea salt flakes and roast for 20 minutes. Pop the hazelnuts on a small tray to toast alongside for the last 10 minutes.

Mix the lemon zest and juice, extra virgin olive oil, almost all the parmesan, 1 teaspoon salt and some freshly ground black pepper together. Once the orzo is out of the oven, stir half this mixture through it. Taste and adjust the salt as needed.

Once the broccoli is out of the oven, dress it with the remaining lemon and parmesan mixture. Divide the orzo between two bowls, top with the broccoli, hazelnuts and remaining grated parmesan. Add a little freshly ground black pepper and serve hot.

DINNER TODAY, LUNCH TOMORROW

Prep ahead with these light dinners that make enough for tonight and for tomorrow's lunchbox. They all reheat well in the microwave, or just take the salads out of the fridge an hour before you're ready to eat.

DINNER TODAY, LUNCH TOMORROW

**THE BEST CAULIFLOWER SOUP,
WITH CHILLI ALMOND BUTTER**
(VEGANISABLE, GF)

**CRISPY MASALA CHICKPEAS,
LEMON DAL & PITTA CHIPS** (VEGANISABLE,
CAN BE GF)

TOMATO, THYME & RICOTTA TART
(CAN BE GF)

**PINK POTATO SALAD WITH RED CABBAGE
& POMEGRANATE** (GF)

BUTTERNUT SQUASH LAKSA (VG, GF)

**ORECCHIETTE WITH CHICKPEAS,
TOMATO & ROSEMARY** (VG)

**RETRO-FABULOUS ORANGE, BUTTERBEAN,
ARTICHOKE & OLIVE SALAD** (VG, GF)

**LIME-SPIKED BLACK BEAN, AVOCADO
& PEANUT BOWLS** (VG, GF)

**BROCCOLI, DATE, PECAN & CHILLI
CHOPPED SALAD** (VG, GF)

**LEMONGRASS, TURMERIC
& TOFU NOODLES** (VG)

**BUTTERBEANS ON TOAST WITH KALE,
LEMON, CHILLI & GARLIC** (VG)

THE BEST CAULIFLOWER SOUP, WITH CHILLI ALMOND BUTTER

Serves: 2 today, 2 tomorrow   Prep: 15 minutes   Cook: 20 minutes

If there's a lonely cauliflower in the fridge, it's almost certain to go into this soup, even if I do have to text a neighbour to borrow nutmeg because Alba's absconded with my jar to use as a rattle. True story. It's hands down my favourite soup – the spiced chilli butter and crunchy almonds finish the dish beautifully (props to my friend Emily Riddle who introduced me to a version years ago). Pack leftovers for lunch with the almonds in a separate container – the butter will melt on contact once you've reheated the soup.

900ml whole milk,
  plus extra as needed
1 large cauliflower,
  cut into medium florets
Good grating of nutmeg
  or a couple of pinches
  saffron threads
50g salted butter
80g flaked almonds
2 tablespoons golden
  linseeds (optional)
1 teaspoon chilli flakes
1 teaspoon sea salt flakes,
  plus extra as needed
Your favourite bread or rolls
  (gluten-free, if required),
  to serve

The Marie Antoinette reference is apt here, because her father-in-law Louis XV was obsessed with cauliflowers – they were grown for him at the kitchen gardens of Versailles for his favourite cauliflower soup, called 'Crème Madame du Barry' after his mistress.

Bring the milk to the boil in a large saucepan with the cauliflower and nutmeg (or use saffron if you have no nutmeg, as Marie Antoinette might say*), and simmer, partially covered, for 15 minutes until the cauliflower is soft. Let it cool for 15 minutes, then blitz with a stick blender until you have a velvety smooth soup. (Or transfer a few ladlefuls at a time to a high-speed blender, then into a clean pan.) Add a splash more milk if you want to thin it.

For the chilli butter, heat the butter and flaked almonds in a small frying pan over a medium to low heat and fry, stirring frequently, for 3–4 minutes until the almonds are golden brown. Stir in the golden linseeds (if using) and the chilli flakes, then turn off the heat.

Reheat the soup until bubbling, then season with the salt; taste and adjust as needed. Pour into bowls, spooning the chilli almond butter equally between them, and serve hot.

VEGANISE: Replace the milk with good veg stock and add 100g ground almonds before blitzing. Season with lemon juice as needed. You may need more stock to thin the soup. Replace the butter with olive oil when frying the almonds.

CRISPY MASALA CHICKPEAS, LEMON DAL & PITTA CHIPS

Serves: 2 today, 2 tomorrow   Prep: 15 minutes   Cook: 30 minutes

There's a wonderful Madhur Jaffrey recipe where she describes a lemon dal made by lining a large bowl with sliced lemons, pouring the cooked dal on top and leaving it to infuse; this simplified version is my homage to that, topped with crisp spiced chickpeas and served with pitta chips to scoop. It's even nicer warmed through the next day – just store in separate containers.

300g red lentils,
  rinsed and drained
1 litre boiling water
½ teaspoon ground turmeric
2 x 400g tins chickpeas,
  drained and rinsed
3 teaspoons chaat masala
2 teaspoons sea salt flakes,
  plus extra as needed
2 tablespoons neutral
  or olive oil
4 wholemeal pitta breads,
  cut into tortilla chip-sized
  wedges
15g salted butter
2 lemons, zest and juice,
  plus extra as needed
2 teaspoons cumin seeds
Handful fresh coriander leaves,
  to garnish

VEGANISE: Use oil instead of butter to fry the cumin seeds and lemon zest.

MAKE IT GF: Use gluten-free pitta bread.

Tip the lentils and boiling water into a large saucepan along with the turmeric and bring to the boil. Cover and simmer for 20–30 minutes until the lentils are completely soft. Whisk until fairly smooth. The dal will thicken as it sits, so be prepared to add a splash more boiling water if needed.

Meanwhile, preheat the oven to 180°C fan/200°C/gas 6. Mix together the chickpeas, chaat masala, 1 teaspoon of sea salt flakes and 1 tablespoon of the oil in a baking tray large enough to hold everything in one layer. Transfer to the oven to roast for 20–25 minutes until crisp.

Mix the pitta bread wedges, remaining tablespoon of oil and ½ teaspoon of sea salt flakes on another baking tray and transfer to another shelf in the oven to crisp up for 15–18 minutes (keep an eye on them – they go from bread to chips quickly).

Heat the butter in a small frying pan over a medium heat until foaming, then add the lemon zest and cumin seeds. Let them sizzle for 30 seconds, then tip the butter in with the lentils. Stir, then add half the lemon juice and the remaining teaspoon of salt. Taste and add more salt and lemon juice as needed. Serve the dal topped with the chickpeas, pitta chips and coriander.

TOMATO, THYME & RICOTTA TART

Serves: 2 today, 2 tomorrow   Prep: 15 minutes   Cook: 40 minutes

This tart is as nice on the day it's made as it is for lunchboxes the next day – even nicer if you can take it outside on the first night, with a glass of rosé and a light green salad alongside. You can use fresh rather than roasted cherry tomatoes if you're in a hurry, but I love the depth of flavour you get from that first brief stint in the oven.

250g cherry or mixed
  tomatoes, halved
2 tablespoons olive oil
½ teaspoon sea salt flakes
2 cloves garlic, finely grated
Handful fresh thyme sprigs
1 x 320g sheet all butter
  (if available) ready-rolled puff
  pastry, chilled
150g ricotta
4 nice free-range eggs
1 lemon, zest only
1 teaspoon sea salt flakes

Preheat the oven to 180°C fan/200°C/gas 6. Pop the halved tomatoes into a roasting tin large enough to hold them all in one layer, then mix well with the olive oil, salt and grated garlic, turning them cut side up. Scatter with the thyme, reserving a few sprigs for later, and roast for 15 minutes.

Once the tomatoes are cooked, line a small, deep roasting tin (20cm by 30cm) with the chilled puff pastry – you want it to come up the sides a little to hold all the filling in.

Beat the ricotta, eggs, lemon zest and salt together, then pour the mixture over the pastry base. Arrange the cooked tomatoes over the top, scatter over the reserved thyme leaves, then transfer to the oven to bake for 25 minutes, after which the centre of the quiche should be firm and the pastry golden brown.

Leave to sit in the tin for 10 minutes to cool down before serving hot or at room temperature.

MAKE IT GF: Use gluten-free ready-rolled puff pastry.

PINK POTATO SALAD WITH RED CABBAGE & POMEGRANATE

Serves: 2 today, 2 tomorrow   Prep: 10 minutes   Cook: 10 minutes

This is one of my favourite potato salads – the red cabbage and pomegranate add flavour, texture and colour to the dish, and you've got all your food groups covered with butterbeans for protein. It's perfect for a light dinner with good bread and butter alongside, and leftovers are excellent in lunchboxes the next day.

600g baby new potatoes, halved
100g mayonnaise
50g yogurt
½ lemon, juice only
3 tablespoons extra virgin olive oil
1 teaspoon sea salt flakes, plus extra as needed
Lots of freshly ground black pepper
½ red cabbage, shredded
200g pomegranate seeds (from 1 pomegranate)
1 x 400g tin butterbeans, drained and rinsed (even nicer if you have jarred butterbeans)
15g flat-leaf parsley, roughly chopped, to serve

Cook the potatoes in a saucepan of boiling water for 10 minutes, or until they're just cooked through. Drain, then rinse under cold water to cool them down.

Mix the mayonnaise, yogurt, lemon juice, extra virgin olive oil, sea salt and pepper together. Taste and adjust the salt in the dressing as needed.

Put the cooled, drained potatoes into a large bowl with the red cabbage, pomegranate seeds, butterbeans and the mayo-yogurt dressing, then taste again and adjust the salt if needed. Arrange on a large plate, then scatter over the flat-leaf parsley before serving at room temperature.

LEFTOVERS: If you're stuck for ideas for using the leftover ½ red cabbage, it's great added to the broccoli salad on page 84.

BUTTERNUT SQUASH LAKSA

Serves: 2 today, 2 tomorrow   Prep: 15 minutes   Cook: 25 minutes

This is a wonderful light meal with plenty of punchy flavours – and it's even nicer the next day for envy-inducing lunchboxes. You can make up larger batches of laksa paste and freeze or refrigerate for future use if you wish.

For the paste
2 banana shallots
2 inches ginger, peeled
2 cloves garlic, peeled
1 inch turmeric, peeled
   (or 1 teaspoon ground turmeric)
1 stick lemongrass, tough
   outer leaves removed,
   then roughly chopped
2 fresh red chillies
1 teaspoon coriander seeds

1 tablespoon neutral or olive oil
500g butternut squash, peeled
   and cut into 1 ½cm wedges
500ml boiling vegetable stock
   (gluten-free, if required)
1 x 400ml tin coconut milk
1 tablespoon soft light
   brown sugar
15g fresh coriander
15g fresh mint
1 courgette, grated
200g rice vermicelli noodles
1 tablespoon soy sauce
   (gluten-free, if required,
   or tamari), plus extra as needed
2 limes, zest and juice,
   plus extra as needed
1 red chilli, thinly sliced

First, make the paste. Combine all the ingredients in a high-speed blender and blitz to a thick paste – use a little of the coconut milk to help blend the paste if needed.

Heat the oil in a large saucepan over a medium heat, then stir-fry the laksa paste for 4–5 minutes until aromatic.

Add the squash, vegetable stock, coconut milk, sugar, half the coriander and mint, then simmer for 15–18 minutes until the squash is just softened.

Once the squash is cooked, add the grated courgette to the pan along with the rice noodles and cook for a further 2 minutes. Add the soy sauce and lime zest and juice, then taste and adjust both as needed. Serve two portions hot, topped with half the remaining mint, coriander and sliced chilli. Divide the rest between two lunchboxes with the remaining herbs and chilli.

NOTE: Increase the amount of stock if you're looking for a lighter consistency.

VEGAN

ORECCHIETTE WITH CHICKPEAS, TOMATO & ROSEMARY

Serves: 2 today, 2 tomorrow   Prep: 10 minutes   Cook: 30 minutes

This lovely Roman-inspired pasta dish is perfect with orecchiette, which catch the chickpeas in the sauce, but by all means use pasta shells or whatever you have in. It's deceptively simple but packs a real punch flavour-wise – just make sure to taste, adjust and taste again to make the dish sing.

2 tablespoons olive oil

1 teaspoon chilli flakes

2 cloves garlic, finely grated

2 sprigs rosemary, leaves
   finely chopped

1 onion, roughly chopped

325g baby plum tomatoes,
   halved

2 x 400g tins chickpeas,
   drained and rinsed

200g baby leaf spinach

300g orecchiette

1 lemon, zest and juice,
   plus extra as needed

Sea salt flakes, to taste

Heat the olive oil in a large, deep frying pan or casserole dish over a medium heat, then add the chilli, garlic, rosemary and onion. Cook for 5–6 minutes, stirring frequently until just turning translucent, then add the tomatoes and chickpeas. Season with a good pinch of salt, stir, then cover and cook for 20 minutes, stirring occasionally. Add the spinach for the last 2 minutes to wilt.

Once the sauce has had 10 minutes, bring a large saucepan of salted water to the boil and cook the orecchiette for 11–14 minutes, or according to the packet instructions, until it's cooked to your liking. Drain well, reserving a mugful of the cooking water, then stir the pasta through the cooked tomatoes, chickpeas and spinach. Add the lemon zest and juice and reserved pasta water a tablespoon at a time to loosen the sauce. Taste and add more salt as needed.

This dish lives or dies by the attention you pay right at the end to the seasoning, so taste, adjust the salt, lemon and pasta water and taste again – you'll be rewarded with a really excellent dinner.

RETRO-FABULOUS ORANGE, BUTTERBEAN, ARTICHOKE & OLIVE SALAD

Serves: 2 today, 2 tomorrow
Prep: 15 minutes, plus 15 minutes marinating   Cook: 10 minutes

This recipe is inspired by Niki Segnit's *The Flavour Thesaurus: More Flavours* – a wonderful resource for anyone who loves food and flavours and wants to know how to put them together. I certainly wouldn't have thought of pairing orange, butterbeans and black olives before but it works perfectly. Here, I add artichokes, walnuts and spinach for retro appeal, flavour and texture. It's perfect for a light dinner and lunchbox on a hot day.

2 tablespoons olive oil
  (you can use the oil from the
  jar of artichokes)
1 orange, zest and juice
50g walnuts, roughly chopped
1 tablespoon coriander seeds
1 clove garlic, finely grated
1 x 700g jar butterbeans
  (or 2 x 400g tins butterbeans),
  drained and rinsed
1 teaspoon sea salt flakes
185g drained jarred artichokes,
  quartered
200g baby leaf spinach
2 oranges, peeled
  and cut into segments
50g black olives, halved

For the dressing
1 lemon, zest and juice
2 tablespoons olive oil
Sea salt flakes, to taste

Heat the oil in a large frying pan over a medium heat and add the orange zest, walnuts, coriander seeds and garlic. Lower the heat and cook for 5 minutes, stirring occasionally, until the walnuts have toasted. Add the butterbeans and sea salt flakes, stir gently, and heat for a further 5 minutes before turning off the heat and stirring through the artichokes and orange juice. Leave to marinate for 15 minutes, or in the fridge until needed.

Once you're ready to eat, whisk together the lemon zest and juice, olive oil and sea salt flakes in a small bowl. Use this to dress the spinach, then stir through the marinated beans, orange segments and olives. Serve immediately.

NOTE: If prepping ahead, remove the beans from the fridge 30 minutes before you eat.

LIME-SPIKED BLACK BEAN, AVOCADO & PEANUT BOWLS

Serves: 2 today, 2 tomorrow   Prep: 10 minutes   Cook: 35 minutes

This is a lovely balanced dinner and next-day lunchbox that takes very little effort to put together. Brown rice, black beans, lime, tomatoes and avocado were made to go together – think of it as a sort of deconstructed guacamole/salsa dish. Serve with tortilla chips and (vegan) sour cream on the side, if you like.

250g brown basmati rice

3 tablespoons olive oil

2 cloves garlic, finely grated

4 spring onions, thinly sliced

300g cherry tomatoes, halved

1 teaspoon ground cumin

2 x 400g tins black beans,
    drained and rinsed

3 limes, zest and juice

10g fresh coriander,
    leaves and stems chopped

2 avocados, sliced

Sea salt flakes, to taste

Handful salted peanuts,
    to serve

Bring a large saucepan of water to the boil, add the brown rice and simmer for 25–35 minutes until cooked to your liking. Drain well, then stir through a pinch of salt and 1 tablespoon of the olive oil.

While the rice is cooking, heat 2 tablespoons of oil in a saucepan over a medium to low heat and add the garlic. Let it sizzle for 30 seconds, then add the spring onions and tomatoes. Stir-fry for 3-4 minutes to soften the tomatoes, then add the cumin, black beans and a teaspoon of salt and warm through for a further 5 minutes. Dress with the zest and juice of 2 of the limes and the chopped coriander; taste and adjust the salt as needed.

Once the rice is cooked and dressed, serve in bowls topped with the beans and sliced avocado. Squeeze the remaining lime over each avocado and add a pinch of sea salt. Serve topped with the peanuts.

NOTE: For lunchboxes the next day, take the avocado to work with you and halve it and add the dressing just before you eat.

BROCCOLI, DATE, PECAN & CHILLI CHOPPED SALAD

Serves: 2 today, 2 tomorrow   Prep: 15 minutes   Cook: 2 minutes

Confession: I'm a lifelong green salad avoider and am generally opposed to raw broccoli (don't get me started on raw cauliflower). But this moreish, substantial salad, inspired by a broccoli dish they serve at the restaurant Dishoom, will have even the most hardened salad sceptics converted – it's packed with colour, flavour and texture and, unusually, tastes just as good the next day in a lunchbox. And, as you'll see, I avoid the raw broccoli issue by quickly blanching it before adding the dressing. Serve with hot flatbreads (gluten-free, if required) and hummus alongside for a filling, colourful dinner.

200g mangetout, halved
   lengthways
1 broccoli, florets thinly sliced
½ red onion, thinly sliced
6 medjool dates,
   stoned and sliced
100g pecans,
   roughly chopped

For the dressing
2 limes, zest and juice
   (you need 50ml juice)
50ml olive oil
1 inch ginger, finely grated
1 teaspoon sea salt flakes,
   plus extra as needed
1 red chilli, thinly sliced

Tip the mangetout, sliced broccoli and red onion into a large bowl, cover with boiling water and leave to blanch for 2 minutes before draining well.

Meanwhile, whisk together the lime zest and juice, olive oil, ginger, sea salt and red chilli for the dressing in a small bowl.

In a large bowl, mix the drained mangetout, broccoli and onion with the dressing, medjool dates and pecans. Taste and adjust the salt as needed, then serve. The colour will be less vibrant the next day, because the lime juice in the dressing dulls the colour of green veg, but it'll taste fabulous.

LEMONGRASS, TURMERIC & TOFU NOODLES

Serves: 2 today, 2 tomorrow   Prep: 15 minutes, plus 30 minutes marinating
Cook: 10 minutes

This is a dish for anyone who likes the idea of leftovers but wants to eat something a little different the next day. The rich turmeric and lemongrass tofu works beautifully with noodles for a weeknight dinner and is even nicer stuffed into a baguette with peanut butter and coriander for a next-day bánh mì-style sandwich.

1cm fresh turmeric, finely grated, or ½ teaspoon ground
2 inches ginger, finely grated
2 cloves garlic, finely grated
1 stick lemongrass, grated or finely chopped (remove tough outer leaves first)
3 tablespoons sesame oil, plus extra to serve
3 tablespoons soy sauce, plus extra as needed
1 red chilli, finely chopped
450g firm tofu, cut into 1cm cubes
150ml water
200g tenderstem broccoli, finely chopped
2 carrots, grated
Sea salt flakes, to taste

To serve
Day one: 2 portions straight-to-wok thick udon noodles, fresh coriander and mint
Day two: 2 nice baguettes, peanut butter, fresh coriander and mint

Mix together the turmeric, ginger, garlic, lemongrass, 2 tablespoons of the sesame oil, the soy sauce and chilli in a large bowl, then add the tofu cubes. Gently stir, then cover and leave to marinate for 30 minutes at room temperature (or longer in the fridge if you're prepping ahead).

When you're ready to eat, heat the remaining tablespoon of sesame oil in a large frying pan over a medium to high heat. Fry the tofu for 2–3 minutes on each side, then add 100ml of the water and 1 teaspoon salt. Let the tofu braise for a further 3–4 minutes to reduce the liquid, then stir through the broccoli, carrots and remaining 50ml water and cook, covered, for 2 minutes.

Remove half the tofu and set aside for your bánh mì tomorrow, then add the straight-to-wok noodles to the remaining tofu. Stir gently for 2 minutes until the noodles are heated through, then taste and adjust the salt and soy sauce. Serve hot, scattered with the fresh coriander and mint and with a final drizzle of sesame oil, if you wish.

The next day, pack the peanut butter baguettes with the tofu in a separate container. Fill the baguettes with the tofu, coriander and mint just before you eat.

BUTTERBEANS ON TOAST WITH KALE, LEMON, CHILLI & GARLIC

Serves: 2 today, 2 tomorrow   Prep: 10 minutes   Cook: 20 minutes

I like to think of this as a sort of deconstructed bruschetta – the marinated lemon and chilli butterbeans piled onto crisp, almost-fried bread makes a lovely light dinner. The beans taste even nicer the next day stuffed into sandwiches, with vegan or ordinary cream cheese and a dash of hot sauce for an extra kick.

3 tablespoons olive oil
2 cloves garlic, thinly sliced
1 teaspoon chilli flakes
   (or less if preferred)
1 lemon, zest and juice
1 teaspoon sea salt flakes,
   plus extra as needed
1 x 700g jar butterbeans
   (or 2 x 400g tin butterbeans),
   drained and rinsed
180g kale, thinly sliced
50ml boiling water

For the toast
As many slices of sourdough
   bread as you like
Extra virgin olive oil,
   for drizzling
1 clove garlic, halved
Sea salt flakes, to taste

To serve
Day two: sourdough bread,
   vegan or ordinary cream
   cheese, hot sauce (optional)

Heat the oil in a large saucepan over a low heat, then add the garlic, chilli, lemon zest and salt. Warm through for 3 minutes before adding the butterbeans. Stir, then leave to warm through for a further 10 minutes, stirring frequently.

Meanwhile, heat a griddle pan or large frying pan over a medium heat. Drizzle the sourdough slices with the olive oil and toast them until crisp on both sides. Rub one side of the bread with the cut garlic clove and a scatter of sea salt.

Once the beans have had 10 minutes, tip them out into a bowl along with all but about a tablespoon of the oil. Return the pan to the heat, add the kale and boiling water and wilt together over a medium heat for 8–10 minutes, stirring frequently, until the kale has softened.

Gently stir the kale and beans together, squeeze over the lemon juice, taste and adjust the salt (important!) and serve warm on the toasted bread.

For lunch the next day, lightly smash the butterbeans and pile into sourdough bread for sandwiches. Add some vegan or ordinary cream cheese and your choice of hot sauce, if you wish.

FAMILY DINNERS

Welcome to the toddler/child-friendly section – where the recipes are flavour-packed enough for you to eat as well (just add sea salt). I'm strongly biased towards things my own 18-month-old will eat – hopefully there'll be some crossover with your children too . . .

FAMILY DINNERS

PANKO-CRUMBED TOFU, WITH TENDERSTEM & PEANUT-LIME DIP (VG, CAN BE GF)

MUSHROOM & LEEK POT PIES (CAN BE GF)

CRISPY BAKED RAVIOLI LASAGNE WITH MUSHROOMS & BASIL PESTO

TOMATO & GINGER DAL WITH BUTTERED SPINACH RICE & JAMMY EGGS (GF)

30-MINUTE MUSHROOM, PEPPER & BLACK BEAN CHILLI (VG, GF)

CHICKPEA, RED PEPPER & TOMATO PASTA

CRISP PARMESAN, OLIVE & SUN-DRIED TOMATO POLENTA BITES (GF)

EVERYDAY CHICKPEA & SPINACH CURRY (VG, GF)

SPELT, CHEDDAR & COURGETTE MUFFINS

ROASTED BROCCOLI, MUSHROOM & COURGETTE PUFFS (CAN BE GF)

BEETROOT, FETA & ROSEMARY MINI MUFFINS

AUBERGINE PARMIGIANA PASTA BAKE

RAINBOW EGG-FRIED RICE WITH SICHUAN PEPPERCORNS (GF)

CRISP PEA & HALLOUMI FRITTERS WITH LEMON & HERB MAYONNAISE

PANKO-CRUMBED TOFU WITH TENDERSTEM & PEANUT-LIME DIP

Makes: many   Prep: 15 minutes   Cook: 15 minutes

We call these 'tofish fingers' at home, and while they're a dish I initially made for Alba, they looked too nice not to try one, followed by three. Adults: try to eat them soon after they come out of the pan, as the tofu has a nice fluffy texture when hot – toddlers seem happy with them at room temperature. Tenderstem broccoli always goes down well, so it's a nice green to serve alongside the moreish peanut and lime dip.

225g packet smoked
   or unsmoked firm tofu
40g smooth peanut butter
40ml water, plus extra
   as needed
40g panko breadcrumbs
200g tenderstem broccoli
Oil, for frying

For the dip
40g smooth peanut butter
1 lime, zest (if you wish)
   and juice
2 tablespoons water,
   plus extra as needed

For you
Soy sauce

MAKE IT GF: Use gluten-free breadcrumbs and gluten-free tamari soy sauce.

Cut the tofu into fingers, roughly 1 ½cm thick. Mix the peanut butter and water together until you have a paste about the texture of double cream (add a little more water as needed). Pour the breadcrumbs into a shallow dish. Dip the fingers into the peanut butter mix, then into the breadcrumbs, turning to evenly coat. Transfer to a plate.

Bring a medium saucepan of water to the boil and cook the broccoli for 4–5 minutes, or until it's the right texture for your child to bite easily.

Meanwhile, heat a little oil in a large frying pan and fry the tofu fingers in batches for about 1 ½ minutes on each side on all four sides until golden brown and crisp. Transfer to a plate lined with kitchen paper.

While the tofu is frying, whisk the peanut butter, lime juice (and zest, if using) and water together for a dip – add a little more water as needed to get a sauce the texture of single cream. You can add any leftover peanut butter from coating the tofu too.

Serve the tofish fingers and broccoli with the peanut and lime dip. Add a splash of soy sauce to the dip for you.

MUSHROOM & LEEK POT PIES

Serves: 4   Prep: 15 minutes   Cook: 45 minutes

This is Alba's favourite pie, because she is a mushroom fiend. Perfect for an autumnal or winter dinner, these little pies are easy to prep in advance – stash the cooked filling in the fridge for up to a day until you're ready to bake. Keep some salt on the table for your portion. These make a lovely family meal with steamed greens alongside.

2 tablespoons olive oil or
   unsalted butter
3 cloves garlic
3 leeks, thinly sliced or chopped
   for fussier children
1 teaspoon fresh thyme leaves
400g chestnut mushrooms,
   roughly chopped
250g full-fat crème fraîche
½ lemon, zest and juice
1 x 320g sheet all butter
   (if available) ready-rolled
   puff pastry
1 nice free-range egg,
   lightly beaten

Preheat the oven to 180°C fan/200°C/gas 6. Heat the oil or butter in a large saucepan over a medium to high heat, then add the garlic, leeks, thyme leaves and mushrooms. Soften for 15 minutes, stirring frequently until the liquid released by the mushrooms has evaporated. Turn off the heat, then stir the crème fraîche into the mushrooms. Season with the lemon zest and juice.

Divide the mushroom mixture between four small pie dishes or ramekins. Stamp out circles of pastry slightly larger than the tops of the pie dishes, brush the rim of each dish with a little of the beaten egg, then stick the pastry lids down. Stamp out shapes or letters of your choice to decorate the tops from the remaining pastry, stick them onto the pastry lids and brush with the beaten egg to glaze. (Save the leftover pastry to make pinwheels with your choice of filling, e.g. cheddar, following the instructions on page 114.)

Cut a small cross in the top of each pie to let the steam out, then put them on a baking tray and transfer to the oven to bake for 25–30 minutes, or until the tops of the pies are golden brown. Let them cool down for 10–15 minutes before serving to children.

MAKE IT GF: Use gluten-free ready-rolled puff pastry.

CRISPY BAKED RAVIOLI LASAGNE WITH MUSHROOMS & BASIL PESTO

Serves: 4   Prep: 10 minutes   Cook: 35–45 minutes

This was my proudest lockdown creation – lasagne made with bought ravioli instead of lasagne sheets – I've made countless versions since. The tinned tomatoes cook down beautifully in the oven with the ravioli, with crème fraîche in place of a béchamel sauce – perfect for a quick and easy dinner. It might seem unusual to put the tinned tomatoes straight into the oven, but trust the process, it works really well.

2 x 250g packets of shop-bought
  ravioli (e.g. spinach and ricotta)
2 x 400g tins chopped tomatoes
1 x tub chilled fresh basil pesto
 (approx. 140g)
250g chestnut
  mushrooms, sliced
2 tablespoons olive oil
250g crème fraîche
Few big handfuls chopped
  or grated mozzarella
  and grated vegetarian parmesan
Sea salt flakes and freshly
  ground black pepper

Preheat the oven to 180°C fan/200°C/gas 6. Tip the ravioli, tinned tomatoes and pesto into a large roasting tin and mix well. Scatter over the mushrooms, then drizzle with the olive oil.

Spread the crème fraîche over the mushrooms, then scatter with the cheese. Transfer to the oven to bake for 35–45 minutes until the top is golden brown and crunchy. Let it sit for 5 minutes before serving hot, with extra sea salt and black pepper on your portion as needed.

NOTE: For a hit of green to cut through the richness, you can serve this with a lightly dressed rocket salad.

TOMATO & GINGER DAL WITH BUTTERED SPINACH RICE & JAMMY EGGS

Serves: 2 adults and 2 children generously   Prep: 15 minutes   Cook: 35 minutes

This is a lovely, balanced two-pan dinner, ready in just about half an hour. I advocate cooking the pan of rice on the stove so you can use the water to both boil your eggs and cook your spinach. Lest it look like I have the world's most adventurous eater, I will admit that Alba goes through phases with dal – she used to love it as a baby, but at the time of writing is very against it (she will, however, happily steal spoons of this rice from the pan. And ask for pieces of butter as if it were cheese).

60g brown basmati rice per adult, plus a small handful per child

4 nice free-range eggs, at room temperature

2 tablespoons neutral or olive oil

1 teaspoon cumin seeds

1 onion, sliced

1 ½ inches ginger, finely grated

1 clove garlic, finely grated

½ teaspoon ground turmeric

250g cherry tomatoes, halved

140g red lentils, rinsed

500ml boiling water

100g spinach, roughly chopped if you wish

25g butter

Sea salt flakes, to taste (for adults)

Bring a large saucepan of water to the boil and add the rice. Return the pan to the boil and cook, uncovered, for 30–35 minutes (the packet says 20, but I find it's never quite cooked enough by then – taste and see as you go). At any point while the rice is cooking, pop the eggs in gently to cook for 6 minutes before transferring to a bowl of cold water. Once cool enough to handle, peel and halve.

Meanwhile, heat the oil in a large saucepan over a low heat and add the cumin seeds. Let them sizzle for 20–30 seconds, then add the onion. Increase the heat to medium, then fry for 10 minutes, stirring frequently, until golden brown. Add the ginger, garlic and turmeric, stir-fry for 1 minute, then add the tomatoes, lentils and boiling water. Bring to the boil, cover and simmer over a low heat for 30 minutes until cooked through.

Whisk the lentils to help break them down, then remove the children's portions before salting yours to taste. When the rice is cooked to your liking, tip in the spinach, prod it into the water with a wooden spoon, then drain the rice and spinach in a sieve. Give it a good shake, then let it sit for 5 minutes before stirring in the butter. Taste and season your portion of rice with salt as needed. Serve the dal and rice, with the jammy eggs on top.

30-MINUTE MUSHROOM, PEPPER & BLACK BEAN CHILLI

Serves: 2 adults and 2 children   Prep: 10 minutes   Cook: 30–40 minutes

This chilli is a brilliant emergency toddler meal, but nice enough that you'd happily down a bowl too. I tend to stick Alba in her at-the-counter step and let her 'help' by putting the chopped vegetables in a bowl for me as I go. Fry off some chilli flakes in oil or butter for your portion if you wish.

2 tablespoons olive oil
2 cloves garlic, finely grated
1 onion, roughly chopped
1 red pepper, chopped
1 yellow pepper, chopped
300g mushrooms, chopped
    or quartered if small
1 heaped teaspoon
    ground cumin
1 heaped teaspoon
    ground coriander
1 heaped teaspoon
    smoked paprika
½ teaspoon ground cinnamon
1 x 400g tin black beans,
    drained and rinsed
2 x 400g tins chopped tomatoes

To serve
Avocado mashed with a little
    lime juice
(Vegan) sour cream or yogurt
(Vegan) cheese
Sea salt flakes
Chilli flakes fried in oil
    or salted butter
Tortillas (gluten-free,
    if required) or rice

Heat the olive oil in a large saucepan or wide, shallow casserole dish over a medium heat and add the garlic and onion. Cook for 5 minutes until starting to soften, then add the peppers and mushrooms. Stir-fry over a medium to high heat for 10 minutes, then lower the heat and add the spices. Stir-fry for 1 minute, then add the black beans and chopped tomatoes.

Increase the heat and bring the mixture to the boil, then simmer over a high heat for 15 minutes until the sauce has reduced (this will be quickest in a shallower, wide-bottomed pan). If you have time, you can let it bubble for another 10 minutes or so, but it's delicious and ready to serve now if needed.

For babies under 1, roughly blend a portion of the chilli in a food processor or high-speed blender if you're serving puréed food. Otherwise, top portions of the chilli with the mashed avocado, sour cream and cheese, adding the salt and chilli oil or butter to your portion. Good with tortillas or rice.

NOTE: Use kidney beans if you can't easily find black beans.

FREEZE: This freezes very well; just defrost in the microwave or overnight in the fridge.

CHICKPEA, RED PEPPER & TOMATO PASTA

Serves: 2 adults and 2 children   Prep: 15 minutes   Cook: 35 minutes

If your child is anything like mine, I'm guessing they'd happily live off pasta with tomato sauce and cheddar cheese day in, day out. This is a lovely veg-and-protein-packed update – you can blitz the sauce for younger children who'd find chickpeas challenging, or keep it whole for older toddlers and children. The vibe is definitely a creamy tomato sauce, but with a view to a more balanced meal. Adding Boursin cheese does wonders for the flavour – use your favourite vegan soft cheese as an alternative.

2 tablespoons olive oil
2 cloves garlic, finely grated
4–5 sprigs fresh thyme,
  leaves picked
1 onion, halved and sliced
3 red peppers,
  roughly chopped
1 x 400g tin chickpeas,
  drained and rinsed
2 x 400g tins chopped tomatoes
300g wholewheat fusilli
1 x Boursin garlic and herb cheese
  (or vegan soft cheese)
Extra virgin olive oil, to finish
Lots of finely grated cheddar
  (or vegan alternative)
Sea salt flakes (for the adults)

Heat the oil in a large, deep frying pan or casserole dish over a medium heat and add the garlic and thyme leaves. Let them sizzle for 30 seconds, then add the onion. Stir, then cover and soften for 5 minutes. (I use this time to chop up the peppers.)

Add the peppers to the pan, stir, then cover and cook for 10 minutes, stirring once or twice. Add the chickpeas and tinned tomatoes, stir, then simmer for a further 20 minutes, with the lid off, stirring occasionally.

When you've got 20 minutes left on your sauce, bring a large saucepan of water to the boil and cook the pasta for 10–15 minutes, or according to the packet instructions. (I find wholewheat fusilli takes ages to cook.) Turn off the heat, add the Boursin cheese and break it up, stirring well so it melts evenly.

Drain the pasta, reserving a mugful of the water, then stir the pasta through the sauce with a good glug of extra virgin olive oil. Add tablespoons of the reserved pasta water as needed to create a silky texture. Season your portion(s) with sea salt, and grate cheddar generously over everyone's bowl.

CRISP PARMESAN, OLIVE & SUN-DRIED TOMATO POLENTA BITES

Makes: many   Prep: 10 minutes   Cook: 30–35 minutes, plus 1 hour setting

These are a great snack to have a stash of in the freezer – children who like strong flavours will love the olives and sun-dried tomatoes (for less adventurous palates, substitute fried mushrooms, roasted cherry tomato halves or just go all out with cheddar cheese – Alba's favourite). Older children might enjoy choosing cutters and stamping out shapes with you – stars are particularly good as they go very crisp at the edges. Snaffle one for yourself to have with a glass of wine.

600ml boiling low-sodium vegetable stock (gluten-free, if required)

150g quick-cook polenta (not a pre-cooked block!)

90g pitted black olives, roughly chopped

90g sunblush or sun-dried tomatoes, roughly chopped

2 tablespoons oil (if the olives or tomatoes came in oil, use that)

50g vegetarian parmesan, grated

Bring the stock to the boil in a large saucepan. Add the polenta and stir continuously for 4 minutes until thickened and just coming away from the edges of the pan.

Add the olives, tomatoes, oil and most of the parmesan and stir for a further minute until well incorporated.

Spoon the polenta mixture into a lined Swiss roll or shallow roasting tin – you want it just under 1cm thick – and scatter with the remaining parmesan. Let the polenta cool at room temperature for 1 hour. Alternatively, if you're prepping ahead, you can refrigerate it once cool for several hours or overnight.

Once the polenta has set, preheat the oven to 180°C fan/200°C/gas 6. Cut or stamp the polenta sheet into shapes of your choice and arrange on a lined baking tray. Bake for 25–30 minutes until golden brown and crisp, then serve warm.

NOTE: These will keep well in an airtight tin in the fridge for a couple of days, to heat through in the oven as needed.

FREEZE: Freeze the cooked bites in a single layer, then bag up and freeze for up to 6 months. Heat from frozen until piping hot.

EVERYDAY CHICKPEA & SPINACH CURRY

Serves: 2 adults and many baby portions   Prep: 10 minutes   Cook: 30 minutes

This recipe is a real storecupboard staple – the sort of curry you can knock out when there's barely anything in the cupboard. Add frozen spinach if you have it, and it's a lovely balanced dinner – this was one of Alba's favourite meals as a 6–12-month-old. We'd happily polish off half of it, while I'd lightly blitz the other half with freshly cooked rice, serve her a minute portion, then freeze the rest in tiny Tupperware boxes. Add in any extra veg if you have it in – mushrooms and peppers work well fried off with the onions.

2 tablespoons neutral
  or olive oil
1 onion, finely chopped
1 teaspoon ground cumin
1 teaspoon ground coriander
1 teaspoon ground ginger
½ teaspoon ground turmeric
1 x 400g tin chickpeas,
  drained and rinsed
1 x 400g tin chopped tomatoes
200ml boiling low-sodium
  vegetable stock (gluten-free,
  if required) or water (keep
  another 200ml in reserve)
150g spinach (fresh or frozen)
10g coriander (fresh or frozen)
½ lemon, juice only
Sea salt and chilli flakes
  (for the adults)
Basmati rice (page 232),
  to serve

Heat the oil in a large saucepan over a medium heat and add the onion. Fry for 10 minutes, stirring frequently, until golden brown. Lower the heat and add the cumin, coriander, ginger and turmeric, stir-fry for 30 seconds, then add the chickpeas, tomatoes and vegetable stock. Simmer for 15–20 minutes until reduced to your liking, adding a little of the reserved vegetable stock if needed. Meanwhile, cook the rice (page 232).

In the last 3–4 minutes, add the spinach and coriander. Turn off the heat once they're wilted, then add the lemon juice. Take out your portion and season with salt and a scatter of chilli flakes if you wish (you can quickly fry the chilli flakes in a tablespoon of oil if you have time), then serve with the rice.

Serve the toddler portion lightly blitzed or mashed, or as is with the rice for older/more confident eaters. For babies under 1 year, make sure the chickpeas are fully blitzed or mashed to avoid choking.

SPELT, CHEDDAR & COURGETTE MUFFINS

Makes: 12 ordinary or 24 mini muffins   Prep: 15 minutes   Cook: 25–30 minutes

These light, ridiculously moreish muffins are on constant rotation at home – I always have a stash in the freezer for on-the-go snacks (and they go well with a glass of white wine if you get peckish late at night too). With a mix of spelt and self-raising flour, they're indulgent but secretly good for you. Serve sandwiched with cream cheese.

2 large or 3 small courgettes,
  coarsely grated
125g cheddar, grated
150g wholemeal spelt flour
100g self-raising flour
1 teaspoon baking powder
1 teaspoon fennel seeds
½ teaspoon caraway seeds
  (optional)
100ml olive oil
150g natural yogurt
1 nice free-range egg
Cream cheese, to serve

*You will need a 24-hole
non-stick mini muffin tin
or a 12-hole ordinary muffin tin.
Use cases if you wish – I just
lightly oil the muffin tin.*

Preheat the oven to 180°C fan/200°C/gas 6. Tip the grated courgettes into the middle of a tea towel, gather the edges together, then twist and squeeze over the sink to remove most of the liquid.

Put the courgette into a large bowl with the cheddar, flours, baking powder, fennel seeds and caraway seeds (if you have them) and stir together. Beat the olive oil, yogurt and egg together and then stir this into the courgette and flour mixture briefly.

Divide the mixture between holes of the muffin tins and bake for 25–30 minutes until well risen and golden brown. Let the muffins cool for 5 minutes before transferring to a wire rack.

Serve warm, with cream cheese. Leftovers keep well in an airtight container in the fridge, or you can freeze them in a bag and defrost as needed in the microwave or on the counter.

ROASTED BROCCOLI, MUSHROOM & COURGETTE PUFFS

Serves: many!   Prep: 25 minutes   Cook: 55 minutes

The idea for these genius puff pastry wheels comes from my friend Abbie Gillgan, shared with our new-mum group when we were despairing of getting any food into our 12-month-olds (I strongly suspect the babies had their own WhatsApp chat going, encouraging each other to refuse every meal we offered them). The solution? Bought puff pastry. It'll tempt even the fussiest child – and this dish is packed with vegetables, so it's practically a balanced meal. Older toddlers will love these as snacks – add salt to the ones you snaffle.

1 small head broccoli,
   roughly chopped
300g chestnut mushrooms,
   roughly chopped
2 courgettes,
   roughly chopped
2 tablespoons olive oil
1 teaspoon dried thyme
   or a few fresh thyme sprigs
175g cream cheese
½ lemon, juice only
50g cheddar, grated
1 x 320g sheet all butter
   (if available) ready-rolled
   puff pastry

MAKE IT GF: Use gluten-free ready-rolled puff pastry.

PREP AHEAD: You can roast the vegetables a day in advance and then keep in the fridge until needed.

FREEZE: Freeze these flat, then transfer to a resealable bag and keep in the freezer for up to 6 months – they'll defrost quickly on the counter.

Preheat the oven to 180°C fan/200°C/gas 6. Tip the broccoli, mushrooms and courgettes into a large roasting tin, then mix through the oil and thyme. Roast for 30 minutes before removing from the oven.

Let the vegetables cool for 10 minutes, then pulse into small pieces in a food processor – you don't quite want a paste, more of a chopped mince-like texture. Stir through the cream cheese, lemon juice and cheddar.

Unroll the puff pastry, spread the mixture evenly over it, then tightly roll into a sausage. At this point you can refrigerate the pastry for 30 minutes if it looks too soft, but I usually just get on and cut it into 1cm slices. Transfer the slices to a lined baking sheet, well spaced apart (you may need 2 sheets), then transfer to the oven to bake for 25 minutes, increasing the heat to 200°C fan/220°C/gas 7.

Take the wheels out of the oven and let them cool on a wire rack before serving warm or at room temperature. They'll keep well in an airtight container in the fridge for 2 days, or you can freeze them (see left).

BEETROOT, FETA & ROSEMARY MINI MUFFINS

Makes: 12 large or 24 mini muffins   Prep: 15 minutes   Cook: 25–30 minutes

Do you need two muffin recipes in one chapter? You do. These muffins are wonderful for children both to make and eat – the vibrantly pink batter is great fun to mix, and the resulting muffins are a perfect, freezable, savoury on-the-go snack. Served warm, they'd also be a fun breakfast option with cream cheese on the side. Just add a good teaspoon of sea salt flakes to the batter if you're cooking for adults or older children.

200g fresh beetroot, peeled and grated
½ tablespoon lemon juice
150g self-raising flour
100g rye flour
1 teaspoon baking powder
1 sprig rosemary, leaves finely chopped
100ml olive oil
150g natural yogurt
50ml milk
1 nice free-range egg, lightly beaten
200g feta cheese, roughly crumbled
Sea salt flakes (if making for adults) and freshly ground black pepper

You will need a 24-hole non-stick mini muffin tin or a 12-hole ordinary muffin tin. Use cases if you wish – I just lightly oil the muffin tin.

Preheat the oven to 180°C fan/200°C/gas 6. Put the grated beetroot into a bowl and stir through the lemon juice, then add the flours, baking powder, a pinch of sea salt (if using) and chopped rosemary. Mix well.

In a separate bowl or large jug, whisk the olive oil, yogurt, milk and egg together. Very briefly stir the liquid into the flour along with half the crumbled feta, just until you can't see any flour and no further – as Nigella says, the less you mix, the lighter the muffin.

Divide the mixture equally between the holes of the muffin tin, then evenly scatter over the remaining feta cheese and add a small grind of black pepper.

Transfer the muffins to the oven to bake for 25–30 minutes until well risen and firm to the touch. Cool briefly on a wire rack, then eat warm. These are best eaten on the day they're made but can be kept in the fridge in an airtight container for 2 days and reheated gently in the oven as needed.

AUBERGINE PARMIGIANA PASTA BAKE

VEGETARIAN

Serves: 4   Prep: 15 minutes   Cook: 35 minutes

I love aubergine parmigiana, but I also love carbs – cue the aubergine parmigiana pasta bake, a happy marriage of both. I've simplified the recipe so the roasted aubergines, mozzarella and parmesan sit on top of pasta in an oregano-rich tomato sauce. It takes just 35 minutes from start to finish, with the oven doing the heavy lifting (of course) for the aubergine – an easy Sunday night dinner with a meal in the fridge for later in the week.

3 aubergines,
cut into 1½cm cubes
4 tablespoons olive oil,
plus extra for drizzling
2 teaspoons sea salt flakes
(optional)
3 cloves garlic, thinly sliced
1 sprig fresh rosemary
2 sprigs fresh oregano
(or 1 teaspoon dried)
2 x 400g tins chopped tomatoes
350g pasta shape of your choice
50g vegetarian parmesan, grated
2 x 125g balls mozzarella,
sliced into half-moons
Handful fresh basil leaves
30g panko breadcrumbs

Preheat the oven to 180°C fan/200°C/gas 6. Tip the aubergines, 2 tablespoons of the olive oil and a teaspoon of the salt (if using) into a roasting tin large enough to fit them all in one layer (you may need to use the tin that comes as an oven shelf – if so, line it with baking paper). Mix well, then roast for 30 minutes until lightly golden brown and cooked through.

Meanwhile, heat the remaining 2 tablespoons oil in a large saucepan over a low heat and add the garlic, rosemary and oregano. Stir-fry for 30 seconds, then add the tomatoes. (If you have a spare vegetarian parmesan rind in the fridge or freezer, chuck that in too.) Increase the heat and bring the tomatoes to the boil, then simmer gently for 20 minutes, stirring occasionally.

About 15 minutes before your pasta sauce is ready, bring a large saucepan of salted water to the boil and cook the pasta according to the packet instructions (10–12 minutes), or until cooked to your liking. Drain well, reserving a mugful of cooking water, then stir the sauce along with half the parmesan through the pasta, adding a splash of the cooking water if needed. Taste and adjust the salt, if using.

Preheat the grill to medium-high. Spoon the pasta and sauce into a large lasagne dish. Top evenly with the sliced mozzarella, then the basil leaves and the roasted aubergine, then scatter with the remaining parmesan and breadcrumbs. Drizzle with a little olive oil, then pop the tin under the grill and cook for 4–6 minutes until the top is golden brown and bubbling – keep an eye on it and turn the dish if needed to make sure the cheese browns evenly and the breadcrumbs don't catch. Let the pasta bake sit for 5 minutes before serving hot.

RAINBOW EGG-FRIED RICE WITH SICHUAN PEPPERCORNS

Serves: 2 adults and 2 toddlers   Prep: 15 minutes   Cook: 30 minutes

I always thought I was good at making egg-fried rice until I followed the suggestions in Angela Hui's excellent memoir *Takeaway* for this ridiculously moreish version (it's a fabulous book for your reading list). I include the microwave method for the rice in the body of the recipe below, so you don't have to turn to page 232 if you're in a hurry. A brilliant 30-minute dinner.

200g basmati or long grain white rice

400ml water

3 ½ tablespoons sesame oil

1 teaspoon Sichuan peppercorns, lightly crushed

2 cloves garlic, finely grated

1 red pepper, finely chopped

1 yellow pepper, finely chopped

1 courgette, finely chopped

150g frozen peas

3 nice free-range eggs

1 tablespoon tamari or soy sauce (gluten-free and/or low-sodium, if you wish)

Sea salt flakes, to taste (for adults)

Put the rice and water into a lidded, microwaveable container – I use a Pyrex bowl and a plate that fits snugly on top. Microwave on a medium setting (so 800W in a 1000W microwave) for 11 minutes for basmati, 13 minutes for long grain white rice, then leave to stand for 10 minutes. Ideally, take the lid off, fluff the rice through with a fork and let it cool down for 20 minutes, but if you're in a hurry, carry on with the next paragraph as soon as the rice goes in the microwave.

Twenty minutes before you're ready to eat, heat 2 tablespoons of the oil in a large wok or frying pan over a medium heat and add the Sichuan peppercorns and garlic. Sizzle for 20 seconds, then add all the veg and stir-fry over a medium to high heat for 7–8 minutes until softened, but with some bite. Transfer to a bowl. Add another ½ tablespoon of sesame oil to the pan and scramble the eggs over a low to medium heat for 3–4 minutes, then transfer them to the same bowl.

Once the rice is ready, add the last tablespoon of sesame oil to the pan, then add the rice and stir-fry it for 2 minutes. Add the eggs, vegetables and soy sauce and stir everything until glossily coated. Take out the children's portion and add salt to taste to yours. Serve hot.

CRISP PEA & HALLOUMI FRITTERS WITH LEMON & HERB MAYONNAISE

Makes: many!   Prep: 10 minutes   Cook: 15 minutes

I came up with the recipe for these lovely light fritters for my BBC *Gardeners' World* column as a way to use up fresh summer peas and herbs. Alba helps me pick peas from the garden, so it's a wonderful garden-to-table recipe to make with her, even if quite a lot of batter ends up on the floor. You can, of course, use frozen peas – these also make a really excellent on-the-go snack or meal for toddlers. I freeze a bag and defrost as needed (see note below).

250g fresh or frozen peas
125g ricotta
75g halloumi, grated
   (use a lower-sodium cheddar
   if you prefer)
2–3 sprigs fresh mint,
   leaves finely chopped
60g plain flour
1 nice free-range egg
Olive oil or unsalted butter,
   for frying
Freshly ground black pepper
   (for the adults)
Lemon wedges, to serve

For the dip
60g mayonnaise
30g natural yogurt
Handful fresh herbs (basil,
   parsley, mint – your choice),
   chopped
½ lemon, zest and juice,
   plus extra as needed

Boil the peas in a saucepan of water for 4 minutes until tender. Drain and refresh under cold water, then mash roughly with a fork and transfer to a bowl. Stir through the ricotta, grated halloumi, chopped mint, plain flour and egg to form a thick batter. Set aside.

For the dip, mix together the mayonnaise, yogurt, chopped herbs and lemon zest and juice in a small bowl. Taste and add more lemon juice as needed.

When you're ready to eat, heat a non-stick frying pan over a medium heat and add a little olive oil or butter. Drop in heaped tablespoons of batter, then fry the fritters for 2–3 minutes on each side until golden brown. Transfer to a plate lined with kitchen paper and continue frying the rest of the fritters, adding more oil or butter to the pan as needed.

Serve the fritters warm, with the mayonnaise and lemon wedges alongside, and with freshly ground black pepper for you.

FREEZE: Freeze in a single layer, then transfer to a bag. Defrost gently in the microwave or in the fridge overnight as needed. (They will no longer be crisp, but toddlers tend not to notice if you sandwich them with peanut butter.)

LIGHT SHARING PLATES

Quick, minimal-cooking, prep-ahead dishes – serve a couple of these with good bread and a nice pudding (no judgement if bought) for a sharing feast. Bakery or shop-bought madeleines, warmed through in the oven and served with chocolate sauce and strawberries, are my usual go-to to finish one of these meals.

LIGHT SHARING PLATES

FENNEL WITH BURRATA, BROAD BEANS & POMEGRANATE (GF)

TURMERIC-FRIED AUBERGINES WITH YOGURT, CHILLI-BUTTER CASHEW NUTS & CORIANDER (GF)

SPICED ROASTED CARROTS & HAZELNUTS WITH SILKY BUTTERBEAN MASH (VG, GF)

LEEK, BALSAMIC & GOAT'S CHEESE UPSIDE-DOWN TARTS (CAN BE GF)

PINE NUT & HERB-TOPPED TOFU WITH PINK PICKLED ONIONS (VG, GF)

LEMONY POLENTA WITH ROASTED CAULIFLOWER, PINE NUTS, RAISINS & CAPERS (GF)

CHICKPEA, HALLOUMI & POMEGRANATE TABBOULEH WITH SPICED ALMONDS (CAN BE GF)

CHAAT MASALA SPICED WATERMELON, TOMATO & CUCUMBER SALAD (VG, GF)

MARINATED BUTTERBEANS & TOMATOES WITH PISTACHIO & SPRING ONION PESTO (VG, GF)

SIMPLY GRIDDLED COURGETTES WITH MINT & PARMESAN (VEGANISABLE, GF)

STRAWBERRY SALAD WITH GRIDDLED HALLOUMI, CUCUMBER & MINT (GF)

WHOLE-BAKED RICOTTA WITH THYME-ROAST JERSEY ROYALS, NEW SEASON ASPARAGUS & LEMON (GF)

FENNEL WITH BURRATA, BROAD BEANS & POMEGRANATE

Serves: 4 as a side   Prep: 15 minutes, plus 45 minutes standing   Cook: 2 minutes

This is such an easy, minimal-ingredient salad – perfect for one of those hot summer days when you just want a couple of cool, refreshing dishes on the table. I served this to friends over the summer with the simply griddled courgettes with mint & parmesan (page 150), the marinated butterbeans & tomatoes with pistachio & spring onion pesto (page 148), good bread and butter and plenty of crémant – a really lovely balance of dishes, all prepped and cooked within the hour.

1 x 120g vegetarian burrata
150g broad beans
  (fresh or frozen)
1 medium fennel bulb
1 smallish orange, zest and juice
50ml olive oil
1 teaspoon sea salt flakes
100g pomegranate seeds
  (from ½ pomegranate)

PREP AHEAD: You can keep the fennel in water in the fridge, and the cooked, double-podded broad beans, pomegranate seeds and dressing in bowls in the fridge until half an hour before you want to serve. Put the salad together at the last minute – remember to take the burrata out of the fridge at least 30 minutes before serving.

Take the burrata out of the fridge to let it come to room temperature. Bring a saucepan of salted water to the boil and add the broad beans. Cook for 2 minutes, then drain and refresh in a bowl of cold water. Slip the broad beans out of their skins (double-podding – it makes such a difference) and set aside.

Use a speed peeler to shave the fennel into wide ribbons straight into a bowl of cold water and let them sit for 45 minutes – the fennel will then crisp up beautifully. (If you try to use it straightaway, it'll be limp and floppy – not ideal.)

Just before you're ready to put the salad together, whisk the orange zest and juice, olive oil and sea salt flakes together. Drain the fennel slices really well, then pop them into a large bowl with the broad beans. Pour over two-thirds of the dressing and gently mix with your hands to evenly coat everything. Gently tip it out onto a serving platter and top with the burrata and pomegranate seeds. Score the burrata into quarters (a bit like you would a jacket potato), then pour over the remaining dressing. Serve immediately.

TURMERIC-FRIED AUBERGINES WITH YOGURT, CHILLI-BUTTER CASHEW NUTS & CORIANDER

Serves: 4 as a side   Prep: 10 minutes, plus 15 minutes standing   Cook: 20–25 minutes

If I had to pick just one recipe in the book that you simply must try, it'd be this one (don't tell the others). I never get tired of fried aubergines and yogurt – it's one of the earliest dishes I learned from my mum, and this version, topped with crunchy chilli-butter cashew nuts, is a total winner. Try it and see.

3 long, thin purple aubergines
   (or 2 ordinary aubergines),
   cut into 1cm slices
1 scant teaspoon ground
   turmeric
20g salted butter
70g cashew nuts,
   roughly chopped
¼ teaspoon chilli flakes
2 teaspoons soft dark
   brown sugar
Oil, for frying
200g Greek yogurt
½ teaspoon ground cumin
Large handful fresh coriander,
   roughly chopped
Sea salt flakes

Rub the sliced aubergines with the turmeric and a scant teaspoon of salt. Set aside for 15 minutes.

Meanwhile, heat the butter in a large frying pan over a medium heat and when foaming, add the cashews. Stir-fry for 5 minutes, watching them closely so they don't burn, then add the chilli flakes, a pinch of salt and the sugar. Stir for a further 2 minutes, then transfer to a plate to cool.

Wipe out the frying pan and add a good splash of oil. Fry the aubergine slices in batches over a medium to low heat for 3–4 minutes on each side until golden brown and crisp. Remove to a plate lined with kitchen paper and continue until you've fried all the aubergines, adding oil between batches.

While the aubergines are frying, stir the Greek yogurt and cumin together in a bowl. When all the aubergines are fried, transfer the slices to a serving platter and top each slice with a spoonful of the yogurt. Stir the chopped coriander through the spiced cashew nuts, then scatter over the yogurt-topped aubergines. Serve immediately.

PREP AHEAD: Cook the aubergines ahead of time and warm through in the oven before topping with the yogurt and cashew nuts.

SPICED ROASTED CARROTS & HAZELNUTS WITH SILKY BUTTERBEAN MASH

Serves: 4 as a side   Prep: 15 minutes   Cook: 55 minutes

I could eat an entire bowl of this in front of the television, but it's really too nice not to share with friends. The carrots roast beautifully with coriander seeds under foil, while the rich, silky butterbean mash takes just 10 minutes to put together. A substantial, flavour-packed dish which is, as my friend Alex Dorgan would say, incidentally vegan.

1 teaspoon coriander seeds
½ teaspoon black
   peppercorns
12 small carrots, halved
45ml olive oil
45ml water
2 teaspoons agave
   or maple syrup
50g blanched hazelnuts, halved
Sea salt flakes, to taste
Finely chopped flat-leaf parsley,
   to serve

For the butterbean mash
90ml olive oil
1 lemon, zest, plus a squeeze
   of juice
1 tablespoon coriander seeds
3 spring onions, thinly sliced
2 fat cloves garlic, finely grated
1 x 700g jar butterbeans
   (or 2 x 400g tins
   butterbeans),
   drained and rinsed

Preheat the oven to 180°C fan/200°C/gas 6. Lightly grind the coriander seeds and black peppercorns in a pestle and mortar, then add them to a medium roasting tin along with the carrots, olive oil, water and ½ teaspoon salt. Cover with foil, then roast in the oven for 40 minutes.

After 40 minutes, remove the foil, drizzle the carrots with the agave or maple syrup, then return to the oven for a further 15 minutes to reduce the liquid and get some colour on the carrots. Put the hazelnuts on a small baking tray and pop them into the oven at the same time to toast.

Meanwhile, put the olive oil, lemon zest, coriander seeds, spring onions and garlic into a small frying pan and warm through over a low heat for 5 minutes – you're not aiming to get any colour on the garlic, so keep the heat down.

Put the butterbeans and the infused oil, spring onions, etc. into a high-speed blender or food processor and blitz until very smooth. Add a squeeze of lemon juice, then taste and adjust the salt if needed. Warm the mash and spoon into shallow bowls, topped with the roasted carrots. Scatter the carrots with a little sea salt, the toasted hazelnuts and flat-leaf parsley and serve warm.

LEEK, BALSAMIC & GOAT'S CHEESE UPSIDE-DOWN TARTS

Makes: 6   Prep: 15 minutes   Cook: 25 minutes

At the time of writing, these upside-down puff pastry tarts are all the rage on social media – I've had a lovely version with fresh apricots and honey made by my schoolfriend Rosie Downes, followed two weeks later by excellent shallot and cream cheese tarts made by my mum, served with a flourish: 'I saw these on an Instagram video!' They're too much fun not to include here as an easy entertaining dish.

2 tablespoons olive oil

4 tablespoons good balsamic vinegar, plus extra to serve

3 leeks, trimmed and sliced into 1cm rounds

2 teaspoons fresh thyme leaves, plus a few sprigs to serve

2 x 120g rind-on slim logs of goat's cheese, sliced

1 x 320g sheet all butter (if available) ready-rolled puff pastry

6 heaped tablespoons full-fat cream cheese

1 nice free-range egg, beaten

Preheat the oven to 200°C fan/220°C/gas 7. Line a large baking tray with baking paper and mentally mark out six well-spaced-out squares where your tarts will sit. (Alternatively, you can draw these in pencil on the paper, then turn it over so you can see the lines without getting pencil on your food.)

Drizzle a little oil (about a teaspoon) on each square, then add a generous splash of balsamic vinegar. Lay nine circles of leek onto each square area, scatter with the thyme, then lay the goat's cheese slices over the leeks. Cut the pastry into six pieces, spread each with a tablespoon of cream cheese, leaving a 1cm border, then place each one cheese side down over a section of leeks. Use a fork to crimp the edges of each upside-down tart, then brush the top with the beaten egg. Transfer to the oven to bake for 25 minutes until the pastry is golden brown.

Remove the tarts from the oven and let them cool for a minute, then use a fish slice to flip each tart over – the oil and balsamic will have caramelised on the leeks and stuck to the pastry, but if any fall off, just pop them back on.

MAKE IT GF: Use gluten-free ready-rolled puff pastry.

Serve hot, with the thyme sprigs and a good drizzle of balsamic on top.

PINE NUT & HERB-TOPPED TOFU WITH PINK PICKLED ONIONS

Serves: 4 as a side   Prep: 15 minutes, plus 1 hour marinating   Cook: 5 minutes

This is inspired by a dish I had at the wonderful restaurant My Neighbours the Dumplings in East London – if you've ever wondered what to do with a block of silken tofu, this is your answer. It's a delicious little sharing plate – serve alongside shop-bought dumplings, gyoza or bao buns for an at-home dim sum night.

350g silken tofu
1 inch ginger, finely grated
1 ½ tablespoons soy sauce
   (gluten-free, if required,
   or tamari)
1 tablespoon sesame oil
1 lime, zest and juice
50g pine nuts
15g fresh coriander,
   roughly chopped

**For the pink
pickled onions**
½ small red onion,
   very thinly sliced
½ lime, juice only
Pinch sea salt flakes

Very carefully slice the silken tofu into 1cm slices and transfer to a small, shallow dish, large enough to fit all the tofu in one layer. Mix the ginger, soy sauce, sesame oil, lime zest and juice together in a bowl, then pour over the tofu. Leave to marinate at room temperature for 1 hour, occasionally turning the pieces over in the marinade.

Meanwhile, prepare the pink pickled onions: put the sliced red onion into a heatproof bowl, cover with just-boiled water, leave it to blanch for 1 minute, then drain well. Pop the onion into a small bowl, then stir through the lime juice and sea salt. Mix well and set aside, stirring occasionally.

Toast the pine nuts in a dry frying pan over a low heat, watching them intently. They will, of course, burn the moment you turn your back, setting off your smoke alarm, etc. so keep a watchful eye – they should take about 6–7 minutes, stirring frequently.

When you're ready to serve, mix the coriander, cooled pine nuts and onion together. Carefully arrange the marinated tofu slices overlapping on a small serving plate and pour over the marinade. Thickly scatter the tofu with the coriander, pine nut and onion mix and serve at room temperature.

LEMONY POLENTA WITH ROASTED CAULIFLOWER, PINE NUTS, RAISINS & CAPERS

Serves: 4   Prep: 10 minutes   Cook: 30 minutes

Pasta with cauliflower, pine nuts and raisins is a popular Sicilian dish; here, I suggest creamy lemon and ricotta-enriched polenta as the base instead of pasta. It's luxurious enough to serve to friends, but easy enough for a quick dinner at home too. The addition of the ricotta gives the polenta a wonderful lightness.

1 medium cauliflower,
    cut into small florets
2 cloves garlic, finely grated
2 teaspoons capers,
    roughly chopped
1 teaspoon sea salt flakes
2 tablespoons olive oil
50g pine nuts
800ml boiling vegetable
    stock (gluten-free, if required)
150g polenta
200g ricotta
1 lemon, zest only
10g flat-leaf parsley,
    roughly chopped

For the dressing
10g flat-leaf parsley,
    finely chopped
1 lemon, juice only
2 tablespoons extra virgin
    olive oil
80g raisins
1 teaspoon sea salt flakes

Preheat the oven to 200°C fan/220°C/gas 7. Tip the cauliflower, garlic, capers, salt and oil into a large roasting tin, mix well, then transfer to the oven to roast for 25 minutes.

Meanwhile, whisk together the ingredients for the dressing and set aside (zest the lemon first and then set aside to use in the polenta later).

Pop the pine nuts on a baking tray in the oven to toast for the final 5 minutes of the cauliflower cooking time. Once the cauliflower is cooked, stir through the dressing and most of the pine nuts and set aside.

Bring the stock to the boil in a large saucepan. Add the polenta and stir for 4 minutes until thickened. Add the ricotta and lemon zest and a little of the parsley, then taste and adjust the salt as needed.

Spoon the polenta into a large warmed serving bowl, then top with the dressed cauliflower. Scatter over the reserved pine nuts and parsley and serve immediately. (Alternatively, you can plate up into four warmed bowls.)

CHICKPEA, HALLOUMI & POMEGRANATE TABBOULEH WITH SPICED ALMONDS

Serves: 4   Prep: 15 minutes   Cook: 15 minutes

This is a beautiful dish. Salty halloumi, pomegranate, spiced almonds, buttery avo and asparagus – I could eat it every day. If you have jarred rather than tinned chickpeas, by all means use those instead, but a quick stint in the marinade will work wonders even with ordinary tinned chickpeas.

300g bulgur wheat
1 x 700g jar chickpeas
   (or 2 x 400g tins chickpeas),
   drained and rinsed
600ml boiling vegetable stock
125g asparagus, sliced diagonally,
   woody ends trimmed

For the spiced almonds
100g flaked almonds
½ tablespoon olive oil
½ teaspoon smoked paprika
1 teaspoon brown sugar
Good pinch sea salt flakes

For the dressing
15g fresh mint leaves,
   finely chopped
15g fresh basil or parsley leaves
   (or a mixture of the two),
   finely chopped
200g pomegranate seeds
   (from 1 pomegranate)
60ml extra virgin olive oil
1 lemon, zest and juice
Couple of pinches sea salt flakes

To serve
225g halloumi, sliced
2-3 avocados, sliced
Lemon juice

Preheat the oven to 180°C fan/200°C/gas 6. Tip the bulgur wheat into a large roasting tin, then scatter over the chickpeas. Pour over the stock, top with the asparagus, then transfer to the oven to bake for 15 minutes.

In a small, shallow baking tray, mix together the almonds, oil, smoked paprika, brown sugar and sea salt flakes, then pop the tray alongside or on another shelf of the oven for the last 10 minutes. While the tins are in the oven, mix the chopped herbs with the pomegranate seeds, olive oil, lemon zest and juice and sea salt flakes to make the dressing.

Heat a griddle pan to medium-high heat and place the halloumi slices on it. Griddle for 1–2 minutes per side until stripey, then remove to a plate. Fluff the bulgur wheat through with a spoon and leave to cool for 5 minutes before stirring through the dressing. Taste and adjust the salt as needed, then serve hot, topped with the avocado, halloumi, spiced almonds and a squeeze of lemon juice.

MAKE IT GF: Omit the bulgur wheat and stock, roast off the asparagus and chickpeas by themselves in olive oil and cook quinoa in your preferred way before dressing with all the other ingredients.

CHAAT MASALA-SPICED WATERMELON, TOMATO & CUCUMBER SALAD

Serves: 4   Prep: 15 minutes

This easy salad is inspired by one of Ruby Tandoh's – we ate versions of it on repeat through a ridiculously hot summer, braving 35°C in the kitchen to grab the watermelon and cucumber before retreating to the front room to sit in front of a fan. Chaat masala is one of my favourite cheat ingredients: it gives you bags of flavour all in one spice blend. You can buy it in larger supermarkets, or in a packet at your local Asian grocery shop (and once you have it, you can use it for the crispy masala chickpeas, lemon dal & pitta chips on page 70). Serve alongside a barbecue, or as part of a selection of sharing plates.

½ baby watermelon,
   cut into 1cm wedges
1 cucumber, cut into 1cm chunks
200g cherry or baby plum
   tomatoes, quartered
1 large or 2 small limes,
   zest and juice
3 teaspoons chaat masala
1 teaspoon caster sugar
1 teaspoon sea salt flakes
Big handful salted peanuts,
   chopped
Handful fresh coriander leaves,
   chopped

Put the watermelon, cucumber and tomatoes into a large bowl. Mix together the lime zest and juice, chaat masala, sugar and salt in a small bowl, then pour it over the fruit and gently stir to mix.

Arrange everything on a big platter, scatter with the salted peanuts and coriander leaves and serve immediately.

PREP AHEAD: Cut the cucumber and keep it in a bowl of water in the fridge, with the watermelon and the dressing in separate containers. Cut up the room-temperature tomatoes and mix with everything else just before serving.

MARINATED BUTTERBEANS & TOMATOES WITH PISTACHIO & SPRING ONION PESTO

Serves: 4   Prep: 10 minutes   Cook: 15 minutes, plus 20 minutes marinating

This dish is inspired by Noor Murad and Yotam Ottolenghi's *Ottolenghi Test Kitchen* books, which first introduced me to the joys of jarred butterbeans. They can be a hassle to get hold of – online is your best bet without an obliging deli nearby – but it's well worth it, because once you've tried these you'll be hard-pressed to go back to tinned. They sit in a simple marinade, with a spring onion pesto to finish the dish – perfect as part of a grazing table for friends with good bread alongside.

60ml olive oil

1 tablespoon coriander seeds

2 cloves garlic, very thinly sliced

½ lemon, zest only

350g cherry tomatoes,
    quartered or halved

1 x 700 jar butterbeans
    (or 2 x 400g tins butterbeans),
    drained and rinsed

For the pesto

2 spring onions

50g shelled pistachios

Big handful fresh basil leaves

60ml olive oil

½ large lemon, juice only,
    plus extra as needed

1 teaspoon sea salt flakes,
    plus extra as needed

PREP AHEAD: You can prep this dish a day ahead and refrigerate the beans and pesto separately. Warm the beans and tomatoes gently in a low oven before serving to wake up the flavours.

Heat the oil in a large saucepan or wide-based casserole dish over a medium to low heat and add the coriander seeds, garlic and lemon zest. Turn the heat down very low and let them sizzle for 1 minute, then add the tomatoes and cook gently for 5 minutes. Add the butterbeans and cook for 5 minutes, if using jarred butterbeans, or 10 minutes if you're using tinned, stirring occasionally. Turn off the heat and leave them to marinate for at least 20 minutes (or longer if you have time).

Meanwhile, pop all the ingredients for the pesto in a small food processor and roughly blitz – you don't want it too smooth. Alternatively, you can chop the spring onions, pistachios and basil by hand and stir in the oil, lemon juice and salt. Let the pesto sit for 15 minutes, then taste and adjust the salt and lemon as needed – it'll be pretty punchy, but this works really well with the beans and tomatoes.

Spread the beans and tomatoes on a large serving platter and dot with the spring onion pesto. Serve at room temperature.

SIMPLY GRIDDLED COURGETTES WITH MINT & PARMESAN

Serves: 4 as a side   Prep: 10 minutes   Cook: 20 minutes

This is inspired by a salad my sister Padmini used to make, albeit with a couple of drops of superlative truffle oil – long finished, never forgotten. It's just as lovely without – courgette responds brilliantly to the intense heat of a griddle (or indeed a barbecue). This is a go-to side dish at home.

1 nice ripe yellow courgette, thinly sliced

1 nice ripe green courgette, thinly sliced

Olive oil, for brushing

2 tablespoons extra virgin olive oil

½ large lemon, zest and juice

30g vegetarian parmesan, half finely grated, half shaved

½ teaspoon sea salt flakes

Mint leaves, to serve

Heat your griddle pan or heavy-based frying pan over a high heat. Brush the courgette slices with the oil, then griddle in batches for about 5 minutes on each side over a medium to high heat until you have nice griddle lines and the courgettes are cooked through.

While the courgettes are cooking, whisk together the extra virgin olive oil, lemon zest and juice, finely grated parmesan and sea salt flakes in a bowl. Gently toss the cooked courgettes with this dressing in a bowl, then transfer to a serving platter. Scatter over the parmesan shavings and mint leaves before serving hot or at room temperature.

PREP AHEAD: The griddled courgettes will quite happily sit on the side for an hour once cooked – just stir through the dressing before serving.

VEGANISE: Replace the parmesan with a vegan version (page 230), omitting the shaved parmesan.

STRAWBERRY SALAD WITH GRIDDLED HALLOUMI, CUCUMBER & MINT

Serves: 4–6   Prep: 15 minutes   Cook: 10 minutes

Can you have too many halloumi recipes in one chapter? I think not. This recipe is inspired by a Waitrose recipe card as interpreted by my mum, and it's completely addictive. I've often found the inclusion of fresh fruit in savoury salads a little suspect, but this combination will definitely convert you, particularly if you use lovely, in-season strawberries during the summer.

½ red onion, very thinly sliced
½ lemon, juice only
225–250g good halloumi
   or manouri, cut into
   quarter slices
250g strawberries,
   halved if large
¾ cucumber, cut into
   large chunks
Large handful fresh mint
   leaves, roughly chopped

For the dressing
2 tablespoons extra virgin
   olive oil
1 tablespoon honey,
   plus extra as needed
½ lemon, zest and juice,
   plus extra as needed
Pinch sea salt flakes,
   plus extra as needed
Freshly ground black pepper

Mix together the sliced red onion and lemon juice in a small bowl and set aside.

In a separate bowl, prepare the dressing; whisk together the extra virgin olive oil, honey, lemon zest and juice, sea salt flakes and freshly ground black pepper.

Heat a griddle pan over a high heat and lay the slices of halloumi or manouri on it. Griddle for about 2 minutes on each side until nicely striped and charred.

Tip the griddled halloumi into a shallow bowl with the strawberries, cucumber, mint and red onion. Pour over the dressing, then gently stir to mix. Taste and adjust the lemon juice, salt and honey to your preference and serve immediately.

PREP AHEAD: You can prep everything other than the griddled halloumi in advance, keeping the cut fruit, onion and dressing separately in the fridge, then cook the halloumi just before serving. Take the other ingredients out of the fridge 30 minutes before you want to eat.

WHOLE-BAKED RICOTTA WITH THYME-ROASTED JERSEY ROYALS, NEW SEASON ASPARAGUS & LEMON

Serves: 4 as a side   Prep: 10 minutes   Cook: 50 minutes

If Jersey royals and asparagus are in season and you're looking for something new to do with them, look no further. A whole-baked ricotta acts as the perfect foil to the crisp, lemony roast potatoes and roasted asparagus spears – perfect with good bread alongside. If you're serving it to friends for brunch, a heap of soft-boiled eggs wouldn't go amiss.

600g Jersey royals, halved if small, quartered if large

4 tablespoons olive oil

2 large cloves garlic, smashed but left unpeeled

Small handful lemon thyme sprigs

400g new-season asparagus, woody ends trimmed or snapped off

200g frozen peas

1 clove garlic, finely grated

1 x 250g tub ricotta

½ lemon, rind peeled with a speed peeler

1 tablespoon extra virgin olive oil

Sea salt flakes and freshly ground black pepper

Preheat the oven to 200°C fan/220°C/gas 7. Tip the potatoes, 2 tablespoons of the olive oil, 1 teaspoon sea salt flakes, the smashed garlic and half the lemon thyme sprigs into a roasting tin large enough to fit everything in one layer. Mix well, then transfer to the oven to roast for 30 minutes.

Meanwhile, toss the asparagus with the frozen peas, 1 tablespoon of olive oil, ½ teaspoon salt and the grated garlic. Once the potatoes have had 30 minutes, add the peas and asparagus to the tin. Make a space in the centre and gently upend the ricotta in the middle. Dress it with the remaining olive oil, peeled lemon rind and sea salt and freshly ground black pepper, then return the tin to the oven for a further 20 minutes, lowering the temperature to 180°C fan/200°C/gas 6.

Once the traybake comes out of the oven, drizzle over the extra virgin olive oil and squeeze over the juice from the lemon you took the rind from. Scatter over a few more lemon thyme sprigs and sea salt flakes before serving.

NOTE: If you have time, pop the asparagus into a bowl of iced water for 10 minutes before roasting – it'll 'shock' the stems and the asparagus will look greener post-cooking.

BIG DISHES, BIG FLAVOUR

These substantial dishes are perfect for casual get-togethers with family and friends, when you want something more robust than sharing salads on the table. I'm particularly fond of the pies (of course), but for something a bit different, try the miso aubergines 2.0 (page 168) or the easy Malai chickpea curry (page 172).

BIG DISHES,
BIG FLAVOURS

SPICED SLOW-COOKED MUSHROOM PIE WITH CELERIAC & CHEDDAR MASH (VEGANISABLE, GF)

MISO BARLEY MUSHROOMS WITH CORIANDER PESTO (VG)

BLACK PEPPER, CARDAMOM & GINGER ROASTED SQUASH WITH LIME & CORIANDER SPIKED BULGUR (VG, CAN BE GF)

MISO AUBERGINES 2.0 WITH KIMCHI, TENDERSTEM & TOFU FRIED RICE (VG, GF)

BUTTERNUT SQUASH RISOTTO WITH CRISPY SAGE & HAZELNUTS (VEGANISABLE, GF)

ONE-TIN MALAI CHICKPEA CURRY WITH PEPPERS & MUSHROOMS (VEGANISABLE, GF)

SPICED ROASTED TOMATO & MUSHROOM BIRYANI PIE WITH CUCUMBER RAITA (VEGANISABLE, CAN BE GF)

CHEDDAR KIMCHI COBBLER (CAN BE GF)

MUM'S DAL MAKHANI (HOUSE BLACK DAL) (GF)

SPICED SLOW-COOKED MUSHROOM PIE WITH CELERIAC & CHEDDAR MASH

Serves: 4–6   Prep: 15 minutes   Cook: 1 hour 5 minutes

This slow-cooked pie is packed with flavour from warming tagine spices; just leave it in a low oven and let it look after itself. Puy lentils add texture to the filling, and a crisp topping of celeriac, sweet potato and cheddar finishes the dish beautifully. My husband put his fork down after finishing this in record time, with the heartening feedback: 'this pie is FIT'. He's not wrong.

550g mixed mushrooms, halved and sliced
1 large onion, roughly chopped
3 cloves garlic, bashed
4 tablespoons olive oil
2 heaped teaspoons ras el hanout
1 large celeriac, peeled and chopped into 2cm chunks
3 large sweet potatoes, peeled and chopped into 2cm chunks
250g cooked vac-packed puy lentils
½ lemon, juice only
30g fresh coriander, finely chopped
100g cheddar, grated
Sea salt flakes and freshly ground black pepper
Buttered spring greens, to serve

VEGANISE: Replace the cheddar with your preferred vegan cheese.

Preheat the oven to 150°C fan. (You will need to use a fan setting to cook the mushrooms and celeriac on separate shelves.) Tip the mushrooms, onion, garlic, 2 tablespoons of the olive oil, 1 teaspoon salt and the ras el hanout into a large pie or casserole dish, mix well, then cover with foil or a lid and bake in the oven for 1 hour.

Meanwhile, mix together the celeriac, sweet potatoes, remaining olive oil, 1 teaspoon salt and some freshly ground black pepper in a roasting tin large enough to hold all the pieces in one layer. Transfer to another shelf in the oven to bake for 45 minutes.

Remove both tins from the oven, then stir the puy lentils, lemon juice and coriander through the mushrooms.

Preheat the grill to medium-high (mine says 200°C). Transfer the roasted celeriac and sweet potato to a bowl and roughly mash with half the cheddar. Taste and add salt as needed.

Spoon the celeriac mash over the mushrooms, then top with the remaining cheddar. Pop the dish under the hot grill for 4–5 minutes, turning the dish as needed so the topping browns evenly. Serve hot, with buttered spring greens alongside.

MISO BARLEY MUSHROOMS WITH CORIANDER PESTO

Serves: 4   Prep: 15 minutes   Cook: 1 hour

This is one of my favourite recipes in the book. The combination of miso, barley and mushrooms is inspired by Niki Segnit's *Flavour Thesaurus: More Flavours*, while the incredibly moreish coriander pesto is my version of Noor Murad's from *Ottolenghi Test Kitchen: Extra Good Things* – a happy melange of inspiration where the pearl barley and mushrooms look after themselves in the oven, leaving you to just blitz the pesto (and bask in the admiration of your dinner guests when they take their first bite).

300g pearl barley, rinsed

750ml boiling water

4 heaped teaspoons white miso paste

1 onion, finely chopped

1 teaspoon freshly ground black pepper

Small handful dried shiitake mushrooms, chopped

300g chestnut mushrooms, thickly sliced

1 red onion, thickly sliced

2 cloves garlic, finely grated

2 tablespoons olive oil

1 x 400g tin haricot beans, drained and rinsed

Sea salt flakes

For the pesto

40g fresh coriander

1 teaspoon coriander seeds

40g pine nuts

80ml olive oil

1 teaspoon sea salt flakes, plus extra as needed

1 ½ tablespoons lemon juice, plus extra as needed

Preheat the oven to 180°C fan/200°C/gas 6. Put the pearl barley, boiling water, miso paste, onion, black pepper and diced shiitake mushrooms in a lidded casserole dish or medium roasting tin, then cover with the lid or foil and roast in the oven for 1 hour.

Put the mushrooms and red onion into another large roasting tin with the garlic, olive oil, haricot beans and a pinch of sea salt. Stir, then pop into the oven for 25–30 minutes until the mushrooms are cooked through.

Blitz the coriander leaves and stems, coriander seeds, pine nuts, olive oil, sea salt and lemon juice in a high-speed blender or small food processor until smooth. Taste and adjust the salt and lemon juice, then set aside.

Stir 2 tablespoons of the pesto through the hot pearl barley, then divide between four plates. Top with the mushrooms and remaining pesto and serve hot.

BLACK PEPPER, CARDAMOM & GINGER ROASTED SQUASH WITH LIME & CORIANDER SPIKED BULGUR

Serves: 4   Prep: 15 minutes   Cook: 45 minutes

Perfect as a sharing dish, the spiced roasted squash works beautifully with the flavour-packed bulgur wheat in this easy entertaining dish (although it's so simple to make, it'd easily work as a batch-cooked Sunday night dish too). Pomegranate seeds for hits of sweetness are a must.

1 teaspoon black peppercorns

6 green cardamom pods,
   seeds only

1 butternut squash, peeled
   and cut into 2cm wedges

2 red onions, quartered

2 inches fresh ginger, finely grated

2 teaspoons ground cumin

1 tablespoon brown sugar

30ml olive oil

1 teaspoon sea salt flakes

200g bulgur wheat, rinsed

400ml boiling vegetable stock

250g tenderstem broccoli

15g fresh coriander,
   finely chopped

½ lime, zest and juice

30ml extra virgin olive oil

200g pomegranate seeds
   (from 1 pomegranate)

For the dressing

60g tahini

1 lemon, juice only

2 tablespoons olive oil

4 tablespoons water,
   plus extra as needed

1 teaspoon sea salt flakes,
   plus extra as needed

Freshly ground black pepper

Preheat the oven to 180°C fan/200°C/gas 6. (You will need a fan oven to cook the squash and bulgur at the same time.) Use a pestle and mortar to crush the peppercorns and cardamom seeds somewhere between coarsely and finely – you want some texture but not great lumps of pepper. Tip them into a roasting tin with the squash, onions, ginger, cumin, brown sugar, olive oil and 1 teaspoon salt and mix well to coat. Transfer to the top shelf of the oven to roast for 45 minutes.

When there's 20 minutes left on your squash, mix together the bulgur wheat and vegetable stock in a small roasting tin, add the broccoli, cover tightly with foil, then transfer to the lower shelf of the oven and bake for 15 minutes.

Meanwhile, whisk the tahini, lemon juice, olive oil, water, salt and a good grind of black pepper together really well, adding more water as needed so you have a dressing the consistency of single cream. Taste and adjust the salt as needed.

After 15 minutes, remove the bulgur wheat from the oven, let it stand for 5 minutes, then fluff through with a fork. Stir through half the coriander, the lime zest and juice, the extra virgin olive oil and half the pomegranate seeds. Mix with the hot roasted butternut squash and onions (just out of the oven), drizzle over the tahini dressing and scatter over the remaining pomegranate seeds and coriander.

PREP AHEAD: You can prep this dish up to a day ahead with the cooked bulgur and squash mixed together – cool and refrigerate, then warm through in the oven and finish with the tahini sauce, remaining pomegranate and coriander just before serving.

MAKE IT GF: Omit the bulgur wheat and cook quinoa in your preferred way before dressing with the lime, olive oil, etc.

MISO AUBERGINES 2.0 WITH KIMCHI, TENDERSTEM & TOFU FRIED RICE

Serves: 6   Prep: 15 minutes   Cook: 40 minutes

Another update on a favourite recipe – I was really missing a trick not adding a pinch of brown sugar to the miso aubergine recipe in *The Green Roasting Tin*. This updated version includes an easy side of kimchi fried rice, which you can make in about 10 minutes while the aubergines cook in the oven – nice enough to serve to friends, easy enough to make for yourself.

1 inch ginger, finely grated

3 cloves garlic, finely grated

3 tablespoons sesame oil

40g white miso paste

1 ½ tablespoons soft dark
brown sugar

3 aubergines, quartered
and scored

For the dressing

1 ½ limes, zest and juice

1 ½ tablespoons sesame oil

1 tablespoon brown sugar

1 ½ tablespoons tamari

1 red chilli, finely chopped

10g fresh coriander,
finely chopped

For the rice

300g silken tofu

3 tablespoons toasted
sesame oil

2 inches ginger, finely grated

2 cloves garlic, finely grated

200g tenderstem broccoli,
finely chopped

Cooked basmati rice (page 232)

3 heaped tablespoons kimchi,
chopped, plus extra as needed

Preheat the oven to 180°C fan/200°C/gas 6. Mix together the ginger, garlic, sesame oil, miso paste and brown sugar in a bowl. Put the scored aubergines in a roasting tin large enough to hold all the quarters in one layer (or use two roasting tins and a fan oven). Evenly rub with the miso mixture, then transfer to the oven to roast for 40 minutes until cooked through.

Meanwhile, whisk together all the dressing ingredients and set aside.

When the aubergines have 15 minutes left, pat the tofu block dry with kitchen paper, then crumble. Heat the sesame oil in a large frying pan and add the ginger and garlic. Let it sizzle for 30 seconds before adding the tofu and broccoli. Stir-fry for 2–3 minutes, then add the rice and fry for a further 3–4 minutes over a medium heat. Turn off the heat and stir through the kimchi. You should be OK for salt, but taste and adjust as needed, adding more kimchi if you wish.

Drizzle the dressing over the aubergines, then serve with the fried rice alongside.

BUTTERNUT SQUASH RISOTTO WITH CRISPY SAGE & HAZELNUTS

Serves: 6   Prep: 15 minutes   Cook: 1 hour

I tested this risotto at home on a very well-known food writer, using a randomly flavoured butter (we'd run out of ordinary – a travesty) as the base for the sage, hazelnut and chilli topping. She thought the combination of the herb-flavoured butter and frying sage made the kitchen smell like marijuana, but asked for the recipe anyway. I can't promise that yours will be quite the same without ancient fridge-raid butter, but this is a spectacular dinner-party dish nonetheless – and easy enough to batch-cook for indulgent at-home autumnal dinners, too. See the note for the easy 7-minute pressure-cooker version.

45ml olive oil

1 onion, finely chopped

3 cloves garlic, finely grated

300g arborio rice

100ml white wine

1 butternut squash, peeled and cut into 1 ½cm cubes

Approx. 1.3 litres boiling vegetable stock (gluten-free, if required)

50g vegetarian or vegan (page 230) parmesan, grated

Sea salt flakes, to taste

For the crispy sage and hazelnuts

30g butter or olive oil

50g blanched hazelnuts

Handful sage leaves

½–1 teaspoon chilli flakes

Preheat the oven to 180°C fan/200°C/gas 6. Heat the olive oil in a large, lidded casserole dish over a medium heat, and add the onion and garlic. Soften for 6 minutes, stirring frequently, then add the rice and stir-fry for 1 minute. Add the white wine and et it bubble for 2–3 minutes before adding the squash and 1 litre of the vegetable stock.

Pop the lid on the dish, then transfer to the oven to bake for 45 minutes to cook through. Remove from the oven and stir through the remaining stock, 100ml at a time (I find I need to add the full 300ml additional stock at this stage for a nice creamy texture), along with half the parmesan. Taste and adjust the salt as needed.

Heat the butter or oil in a small frying pan; when foaming add the hazelnuts, sage leaves and chilli flakes. Cook over a low heat for 2–4 minutes until the hazelnuts are lightly toasted and the sage leaves are crisp. Serve the risotto in warmed bowls, with the crispy sage and hazelnut butter or oil and the remaining parmesan at the table.

NOTE: You can also make this in just 7 minutes in a pressure cooker: follow the instructions in the first paragraph albeit with 750ml stock, then lock your pressure cooker and bring to maximum pressure. Reduce the heat and cook for 7 minutes. If you don't have an electric pressure cooker with a release function, carefully hold the base and sides of the pan under a cold running tap until the pressure releases. Adjust with extra stock, parmesan and salt as required, and prepare the crispy sage and hazelnuts as per the method.

ONE-TIN MALAI CHICKPEA CURRY WITH PEPPERS & MUSHROOMS

Serves: 4 generously   Prep: 15 minutes   Cook: 55 minutes

This is one of my £1-per-portion recipes written for the *Guardian*, a favourite chickpea curry. Everything cooks in one tin in the oven – just look at how short that method is! Packed with flavour, the single cream adds richness and rounds off the fragrant spices. Serve to friends with freshly cooked basmati rice, flatbreads and shop-bought samosas and pakoras (have a look in *India Express* if you fancy making your own), and you'll have a feast.

2 tablespoons oil
1 onion, roughly chopped
1 green pepper,
   roughly chopped
250g chestnut mushrooms,
   roughly chopped
2 teaspoons ground cumin
1 heaped teaspoon ground
   coriander
½ teaspoon ground turmeric
1 teaspoon ground ginger
1 teaspoon chilli flakes
   (or less to taste)
1 teaspoon sea salt flakes,
   plus extra as needed
1 x 400g tin chickpeas,
   drained and rinsed
2 x 400g tins chopped tomatoes
150ml single cream
Basmati rice (page 232)
   or flatbreads (gluten-free,
   if required), to serve

Preheat the oven to 180°C fan/200°C/gas 6. Tip the oil, onion, pepper, mushrooms, spices and salt into a large roasting tin, then mix well. Transfer to the oven to roast for 15 minutes.

Remove the tin from the oven, stir through the chickpeas, chopped tomatoes and cream, then return to the oven for a further 40 minutes. Let the curry stand for 5 minutes, then taste and adjust the salt as needed. Serve hot with rice or flatbreads.

VEGANISE: Omit the single cream and stir through several generous spoonfuls of coconut yogurt just before serving.

SPICED ROASTED TOMATO & MUSHROOM BIRYANI PIE WITH CUCUMBER RAITA

Serves: 4   Prep: 15 minutes   Cook: 30 minutes

This is a lovely special-occasion centrepiece – perfect with the raita alongside, but it also works really well with the dal makhani on page 180, which you can make the day before. There's some alchemy when the spiced vegetables and rice cook in layers in the oven, and I finish the dish with a crisp sheet of puff pastry, as a nod to the traditional dough-paste used to seal a biryani pot. Who doesn't love double carbs? Just be sure to use the nicest saffron you can find – Belazu is my favourite supermarket brand.

300g basmati rice
2 tablespoons milk
Generous pinch saffron threads
25g butter
300g cherry tomatoes, halved
400g chestnut mushrooms,
   thickly sliced
2 inches ginger, finely grated
2 cloves garlic, finely grated
2 teaspoons ground cumin
2 teaspoons freshly ground
   coriander seeds
½ teaspoon ground turmeric
3 cloves, ground
5 cardamom pods, bashed
1 tablespoon neutral or olive oil
150g natural yogurt
1 nice free-range egg, beaten
1 x 320g sheet all butter
   (if available) ready-rolled
   puff pastry
1 teaspoon nigella seeds
Sea salt flakes

For the raita

4 heaped tablespoons natural yogurt
¼ cucumber, seeds removed and
   coarsely grated, then lightly
   squeezed in a tea towel
½ small clove garlic, finely grated
1 teaspoon ground cumin
Pinch sea salt flakes, plus
   extra as needed

Tip the rice into a saucepan of boiling water and par-boil for 8 minutes. Meanwhile, heat the milk for 20 seconds in a mug in the microwave or briefly in a small pan, then add the saffron and leave it to infuse. Drain the rice well, then add 1 teaspoon salt, the butter and half the saffron milk and stir well.

Preheat the oven to 200°C fan/180°C/gas 6. Mix together the cherry tomatoes, mushrooms, ginger, garlic, cumin, coriander, turmeric, cloves, cardamom pods, oil and yogurt in a large bowl with 1 teaspoon salt.

Layer the rice and spiced vegetables in a medium, deep casserole dish, finishing with a layer of rice. Pour over the remaining saffron milk. Brush the edges of the casserole dish with a little beaten egg, then unroll the puff pastry over the dish and trim it to size. Brush with a little more beaten egg, then scatter with the nigella seeds. Transfer to the oven to bake for 30 minutes until the pastry is golden brown and crisp.

While the biryani is cooking, mix together the yogurt, grated cucumber, garlic, cumin and salt in a bowl. Taste and adjust the salt as needed, then set aside. Serve the biryani hot, with the raita alongside.

VEGANISE: Replace the butter with oil or your preferred plant-based spread and the yogurt with coconut yogurt. Most brands of puff pastry (e.g. Jusrol) are vegan: brush with plant-based milk to glaze instead of egg.

MAKE IT GF: Use gluten-free ready-rolled puff pastry.

CHEDDAR KIMCHI COBBLER

Serves: 4   Prep: 15 minutes   Cook: 55 minutes

This is a lovely cultural mishmash of a dish – perfect for an autumnal dinner with friends. You roast fennel, leeks and onion in the oven with classic Korean kimchi seasonings, then top them with a rich, savoury custard, cheddar and bread mixture – it crisps up beautifully in the oven. Korean red pepper flakes are readily available online, but you could substitute with smoked paprika and chipotle chilli flakes if needed. Serve with a crunchy green salad alongside.

2 small leeks, thinly sliced
2 fennel bulbs, thinly sliced
1 onion, thinly sliced
4 cloves garlic, finely grated
2 inches ginger, finely grated
2 tablespoons sesame oil
2 tablespoons Korean
  red pepper flakes (gochugaru)
200g spring greens, thinly sliced
400ml crème fraîche
200ml milk
2 nice free-range eggs
1 teaspoon sea salt flakes
75g cheddar, grated
1 tablespoon soy sauce
300g baguette, sliced
  or torn into pieces

Preheat the oven to 180°C fan/200°C/gas 6. Tip the leeks, fennel, onion, garlic, ginger, sesame oil and red pepper flakes into a large roasting tin, mix well, then transfer to the oven to cook for 30 minutes.

Meanwhile, tip the spring greens into a large heatproof bowl, cover with just-boiled salted water and let them stand for 3 minutes before draining well, squeezing them dry with kitchen paper if needed. Whisk the crème fraîche, milk, eggs and salt together in a large bowl, stir through half the cheddar and set aside.

Once the vegetables have had 30 minutes, remove the tin from the oven and increase the temperature to 200°C fan/220°C/gas 7. Stir the blanched spring greens, soy sauce and half the cheese sauce through the cooked vegetables.

Tip the bread into the bowl with the remaining cheese sauce and stir well to coat. Arrange the bread evenly over the vegetables in the tin and pour over any leftover mixture. Scatter the remaining cheddar over and bake for 20–25 minutes until golden brown and crisp. Serve hot.

MAKE IT GF: Use gluten-free bread and tamari.

MUM'S DAL MAKHANI (HOUSE BLACK DAL)

Serves: 6 generously
Prep: 10 minutes, plus overnight soaking   Cook: 1 hour 20 minutes

I didn't realise until we made this dal together why dal makhani (which you might have had at Dishoom or other Indian restaurants as 'house black dal') is quite so addictive – it's got half a block of butter in, as well as cream. With a mild nod to saving your and my arteries, I've slightly reduced the amount of butter to no ill effect. This really is a lovely one to have in your repertoire or stashed in the freezer, and it's very little effort to make. If you have a pressure cooker, see the note opposite – it'll considerably reduce the cooking time. Do remember to soak the lentils the night before.

300g whole black lentils
  (black urad dal)
1.5 litres boiling water
100g salted butter
4 cloves garlic, finely grated
3 inches ginger, finely grated
1 teaspoon chilli flakes
4 cloves
1 bay leaf
4 green cardamom pods,
  bashed
1 teaspoon freshly ground
  black pepper
1 x 400g tin chopped tomatoes
150ml single cream
30g fresh coriander, roughly
  chopped
Sea salt flakes, to taste

PRESSURE COOK: If you
have a pressure cooker, do
the lentils in that. It'll take 7–8
minutes on a high pressure;
then just turn off the heat
and leave it until the pressure
releases naturally.

The night before you want to cook, pop the
lentils in a large bowl and cover with plenty of
cold water. Cover and set aside.

The next day, drain the soaked lentils, pop
them into a big stockpot, then add the boiling
water. Bring to the boil, then cook at a rolling
boil, partially covered, for 1 hour until mashable
– when you mash the lentils with a fork against
a plate, they should smash easily, and not taste
too raw (they will get another 20 minutes later).
Use a potato masher to mash the lentils in the
cooking liquid until coarsely mashed.

While the lentils are cooking, heat the butter in
a large saucepan; once foaming, add the garlic,
ginger and spices. Stir-fry for a minute, then add
the tomatoes. Bring to the boil, lower the heat
and simmer for 20 minutes until well reduced.

At this point, Mum says you really should blitz
the tomato sauce to blend in the whole spices.
I'll be controversial and say you could just mash
it lightly with a potato masher and fish out the
whole spices with a spoon if they're going to
bother you.

Add the tomatoes, single cream and half the
chopped coriander to the lentils. Bring to the
boil, then reduce the heat and simmer for
20 minutes. Add a little boiling water if you prefer
a less thick dal, then taste and adjust the salt
as needed. Serve hot, scattered with the
remaining coriander. Great made in advance for
the next day.

BATCH COOK

Some for Sunday night, some for the week ahead. Think big pots of pasta sauce, dal, chilli and curry – these dishes all lend themselves to batch-cooking. I've marked out the ones that freeze particularly well too.

7

DATE

CONTENTS

Aubergine, Caper + tom Sauce

BATCH COOK

CRISPY LEEK, CHEDDAR & MUSTARD
LOADED POTATOES (CAN BE GF)

ONE-POT PASTA WITH PEPPERS
& HARISSA (VG)

CRISPY-TOPPED ARTICHOKE,
BUTTERNUT SQUASH & ROSEMARY
BAKED GNOCCHI (CAN BE GF)

SLOW-COOKED ROSEMARY & RED WINE
MUSHROOM RAGU (VG, GF)

ONE-TIN PASTA SAUCE WITH AUBERGINES,
TOMATOES, CAPERS & PINE NUTS (VG, GF)

COCONUT DAL WITH ROASTED SWEET POTATOES
& CHILLI-LIME PICKLED ONIONS (VG, GF)

SPANISH-STYLE CHICKPEAS
WITH GARLIC & SPINACH (VG, CAN BE GF)

ULTIMATE BEAN CHILLI
WITH WALNUTS & CHOCOLATE (VG, GF)

ALL-IN-ONE SMOKY AUBERGINE & PEPPER
TAGINE WITH HALLOUMI CROUTONS
(VEGANISABLE, GF)

CRISPY LEEK, CHEDDAR & MUSTARD LOADED POTATOES

Serves: 6   Prep: 15 minutes   Cook: 1 hour

I can't reread this recipe without wanting to make it immediately – it's the ultimate comfort food, with the perfect ratio of crunch, carb and cheese. And you can stash whatever you don't eat on the day in the freezer for thoroughly indulgent future ready-meals – a total win. This recipe originally appeared in the *Guardian* as part of their £1-per-portion series, so I was keen to minimise the amount of time you'd have to keep the oven on – you can, of course, cook the potatoes the traditional way for an hour in the oven (particularly if you're cooking something else in there too), but the microwave cuts your cooking time and fuel bills if not.

6 large baking potatoes,
   stabbed with a fork
1 ½ tablespoons olive oil,
   plus extra for drizzling
45g butter
3 leeks, thinly sliced
150g mature cheddar, grated
3 teaspoons Dijon mustard,
   plus extra as needed
150ml double cream
Few big handfuls
   white breadcrumbs
Sea salt flakes and freshly
   ground black pepper

Rub the potatoes with a little oil and salt, then place on a microwaveable plate. Microwave on high for 10 minutes, turn the potatoes over, then microwave for a further 10 minutes. Continue in 2 to 4 minute blasts until cooked.

Meanwhile, heat a tablespoon of the butter in a large frying pan with the oil over a low to medium heat, and add the leeks. Stir, then cover and cook for 10 minutes, stirring frequently, until softened.

Preheat the oven to 180°C fan/200°C/gas 6. Once the potatoes are cooked, carefully halve them and scoop out almost all the flesh from the skin, leaving a neat shell. Place the shells cut side down on a lined baking sheet, drizzle with oil and place in the oven while you continue with the filling.

Mix the mashed potato with the softened leeks, 100g of the cheddar, the mustard and double cream. Taste and season with salt, pepper and more mustard as needed. Remove the shells from the oven, turn them over, and divide the potato and leek mixture equally between them. (They will pile up quite high, that's fine.) Scatter over the remaining cheddar, the breadcrumbs and a good grind of black pepper, then return to the oven for 30 minutes until the tops are golden brown. Serve hot.

FREEZE: Freeze the cooked potatoes in one layer on a tray; when frozen, pop them in a bag. These will keep for up to 6 months. Bake from frozen until piping hot.

MAKE IT GF: Use gluten-free breadcrumbs to top.

ONE-POT PASTA WITH PEPPERS & HARISSA

Serves: 4-5   Prep: 15 minutes   Cook: 35 minutes

I'm new to one-pot stovetop pasta, but was instantly converted by the texture and flavour of this dish. As the pasta releases starch into the water as it cooks, you're left with an incredibly rich, creamy sauce – perfect for a vegan dish that involves no cream or cheese. It works perfectly here with the spicy harissa and jammy cooked peppers – try it and see.

3 tablespoons olive oil
4 cloves garlic, finely grated
4 mixed peppers (not green),
   chopped
400g cherry tomatoes, halved
4 heaped tablespoons good
   rose harissa paste
   (I like Belazu)
800ml boiling vegetable stock
400g macaroni
2 lemons, juice only
Sea salt flakes, to taste

Heat the oil in a large saucepan or casserole dish and add the garlic and peppers. Soften over a medium heat, stirring frequently, for 10 minutes before adding the tomatoes. Cook for a further 5 minutes, then add the harissa and stir-fry for 30 seconds.

Add the stock and pasta, then bring to the boil. Lower the heat, then cover and simmer for about 10–15 minutes, making sure to stir the pot every few minutes. If the pasta is drying out too much, add a splash of boiling water. Once the pasta is done to your liking, add half the lemon juice, then taste and adjust the salt and add more lemon as needed. Serve hot.

CRISPY-TOPPED ARTICHOKE, BUTTERNUT SQUASH & ROSEMARY BAKED GNOCCHI

Serves: 4–6   Prep: 15 minutes   Cook: 55 minutes

Could I write a cookbook without including at least one crispy baked gnocchi dish? I could not. This version includes some of my favourite autumnal ingredients – goat's cheese, artichokes and butternut squash. It's just what you want to eat on a cold evening – and leftovers warm through beautifully in the oven the next day.

1kg butternut squash, peeled and cut into 1 ½cm cubes
1 sprig rosemary, leaves chopped, plus a few extra sprigs for the top
1 teaspoon chilli flakes
1 ½ tablespoons olive oil (you can use the oil from the artichoke jar), plus extra for drizzling
1kg potato gnocchi (fresh or vac-packed)
500g crème fraîche
185g quartered artichokes in oil, drained
2 x 125g logs goat's cheese, sliced
Big handful panko breadcrumbs
50g pine nuts
Sea salt flakes and freshly ground black pepper

Preheat the oven to 180°C fan/200°C/gas 6. Tip the butternut squash, rosemary, chilli flakes, olive oil and 1 teaspoon salt into a large, deep roasting tin. Mix well, then transfer to the oven to bake for 25 minutes until just softening.

Meanwhile, place the gnocchi into a large heatproof bowl and pour over a kettleful of just-boiled water. Leave to sit for 2 minutes to blanch, then drain well.

Once the squash has had 25 minutes in the oven, remove the tin and gently stir through the gnocchi, crème fraîche and another teaspoon of salt until evenly mixed. (It doesn't matter that the gnocchi won't sit all in one layer, as this is a gratin-style dish.)

Scatter over the artichoke quarters, goat's cheese slices, panko breadcrumbs, pine nuts, a good grind of freshly ground black pepper and some rosemary sprigs. Drizzle with a little olive oil, then transfer to the oven to bake for 30 minutes until golden brown and crisp. Serve hot.

MAKE IT GF: Use gluten-free gnocchi and breadcrumbs.

SLOW-COOKED ROSEMARY & RED WINE MUSHROOM RAGU

Serves: 6   Prep: 15 minutes   Cook: 1 hour 30 minutes

My husband thinks this is hands down the best vegetarian ragu he's ever had, and our toddler Alba, who usually only eats pasta by carefully scraping off any sauce, will eat this by the bowlful – it's that good. The sauce freezes really well too, so it's perfect for those just-back-from-holiday moments when you're starving and there's nothing in the fridge for dinner. Top with vegan (page 230) or veggie parmesan and you've got an instant feast.

2 tablespoons olive oil
2 onions, finely chopped
3 cloves garlic, finely grated
3 sprigs rosemary
900g chestnut mushrooms
300ml good red wine
3 x 400g tins good tomatoes
   (I like Mutti, finely chopped)
Leftover vegetarian parmesan
   rind (if you have one/are
   not vegan)
Sea salt flakes, to taste

To serve
Your choice of pasta
   (gluten-free, if required)
Vegan (page 230) or vegetarian
   parmesan shavings

NOTE: I've informally checked with GP friends who are also mothers, and they are happy to serve recipes like this to their children, as all the alcohol in the wine has cooked off. If you'd rather not, then just omit the wine – it's still delicious.

Heat the oil in a very large heavy-based saucepan or stockpot over a medium to low heat. Add the onions, garlic and rosemary and cook for 10 minutes, stirring occasionally, until well softened.

Meanwhile, blitz the mushrooms in a food processor until you have a mince-like texture – alternatively, you can chop them by hand, but it will take a while, so consider delegating.

Add the mushroom mince to the onions and cook down over a medium heat for 15 minutes, stirring occasionally, until the water has cooked off. Add the red wine, bring to the boil and simmer for 10 minutes until the liquid has reduced by two-thirds.

Add the tinned tomatoes and parmesan rind (if using), bring to the boil, then reduce the heat and simmer uncovered for 45 minutes to 1 hour if you have time, until nice and thick. If it isn't reducing as you would like, increase the heat. Remove however much any resident children might eat, then generously season the rest with salt, tasting and adjusting as needed. Serve hot, with the pasta of your choice (which you'll have cooked 10 minutes before the sauce was ready) and plenty of vegan or vegetarian parmesan.

ONE-TIN PASTA SAUCE WITH AUBERGINES, TOMATOES, CAPERS & PINE NUTS

Serves: 6   Prep: 20 minutes   Cook: 35 minutes

Two of my favourite Delia recipes involve cubed fried aubergine, tomatoes and mozzarella: one is a pasta sauce from Delia's *Vegetarian Collection*; the other is the griddled aubergine, mozzarella and caper involtini from her *Winter Collection* (which also has the most incredible recipes for chocolate bread and butter pudding and roast potatoes. I'm hungry just thinking about them). Anyway, this recipe is my homage to both, but in one-tin oven form, perfect for batch-cooking. Add your favourite cheese or vegan cheese
if you wish.

4 aubergines,
  cut into 1cm cubes
1kg cherry tomatoes
  on the vine
4 sprigs rosemary
  (or use ½ teaspoon dried)
Few sprigs fresh thyme
  (or use ½ teaspoon dried)
4 cloves garlic, finely grated
4 tablespoons olive oil
2 teaspoons sea salt flakes,
  plus extra as needed
50g pine nuts
50g baby capers, drained

To serve
Your choice of pasta
  (gluten-free, if required)
Vegan (page 230)
  or vegetarian parmesan

Preheat the oven to 180°C fan/200°C/gas 6 – you will need to use a fan oven if you want to cook everything at the same time, as you'll be using two of your largest roasting tins to fit everything in. Otherwise, pop the second tin in after the first.

Divide all the ingredients other than the pine nuts and capers evenly between two large roasting tins and mix well, then transfer to the oven to roast for 25 minutes. Remove from the oven and scatter over the pine nuts and capers, then return to the oven for a further 10 minutes until the aubergines are cooked through and the pine nuts are lightly browned. Remove the cherry tomato vines and squash the tomatoes.

While the sauce is in the oven, cook as much pasta as you need (I use about 80g per person, you might be hungrier and do 100g) in plenty of boiling, salted water. Once cooked, drain well, reserving a mugful or two of the pasta water. Return the pasta to the pan and stir through as much sauce as you need. Taste and adjust the salt as needed, adding tablespoons of pasta water until you have a silky texture. Serve hot, with vegan or vegetarian parmesan and refrigerate or freeze the remaining sauce for another day.

COCONUT DAL WITH ROASTED SWEET POTATOES & CHILLI-LIME PICKLED ONIONS

Serves: 6   Prep: 20 minutes   Cook: 45 minutes

Dal was made for batch-cooking, and this exceptionally nice version, topped with roasted tamarind sweet potatoes and bright pink pickled onions is just as good (if not better) on day two. I use a mix of red lentils, for creaminess, and green lentils, because they keep their shape nicely while they cook, but you could use just one type if you wish. This freezes very well too – stash separately in the freezer for a future emergency dinner.

1.2kg sweet potatoes, peeled
    and cut into 2 ½cm chunks
3 tablespoons olive oil
2 teaspoons ground ginger
2 teaspoons ground cumin
60g tamarind paste
Sea salt flakes, to taste
Fresh coriander leaves, to serve

For the dal
140g red lentils, rinsed
260g green lentils, rinsed
2 x 400ml tins coconut milk
1.2 litres boiling water
Pinch ground turmeric
1–2 limes, juice only

For the pickled onions
1 red onion, halved
    and very thinly sliced
1 lime, juice only
½ teaspoon sea salt flakes
¼ teaspoon chilli flakes

FREEZE: Defrost and reheat the dal on the stove, and the sweet potatoes in the microwave or oven.

Preheat the oven to 200°C fan/220°C/gas 7. Tip the sweet potatoes, olive oil, ginger, cumin, tamarind paste and 1 teaspoon salt into a roasting tin large enough to just hold everything in one layer, then mix well. Transfer to the oven to roast for 35–45 minutes until the sweet potatoes are soft. Taste one and scatter with more salt as needed.

While the sweet potatoes are cooking, tip the lentils, coconut milk, water and turmeric into a saucepan, bring to the boil, then lower the heat and simmer, partially covered, for 40 minutes.

Tip the sliced red onion into a heatproof bowl, cover with just-boiled water and let it sit for 1 minute before draining well. Mix with the lime juice, salt and chilli flakes and set aside to pickle.

Once the lentils are soft, stir through the lime juice and taste and adjust the salt as needed. Serve in shallow bowls, topped with the roasted sweet potato, pickled onions and coriander leaves. Store the remaining dal, sweet potatoes and pickled onions in containers in the fridge and serve hot within 2 days.

SPANISH-STYLE CHICKPEAS WITH GARLIC & SPINACH

Serves: 4   Prep: 15 minutes   Cook: 20–30 minutes

This is a lovely Andalusian tapas dish, in which simply cooked chickpeas and spinach are enriched with a gorgeous toasted garlic picada – fried bread, pounded (or blitzed, if you're me) with garlic, spices and salt. It's rich and moreish, and perfect on rounds of fried or toasted bread – bottle of good red wine/jug of sangria optional. As always, if you can get hold of jarred chickpeas rather than tinned this will be even nicer, but just increase the cooking time fractionally for tinned and it'll be just as good – and, of course, even nicer the next day.

120g stale, firm bread
   (e.g. leftover sourdough),
   crusts removed
2 tablespoons olive oil
5 cloves garlic, finely grated
1 teaspoon ground cumin
2 teaspoons paprika, plus
   a pinch to serve
30ml sherry or white wine vinegar
2 x 700g jars chickpeas
   (or 4 x 400g tins chickpeas),
   drained (reserving 200ml
   of the water) and rinsed
200g spinach, roughly chopped
400ml just-boiled water
Sea salt flakes, to taste
Many rounds of toast
   or lightly fried sourdough,
   to serve
Extra virgin olive oil, to serve

NOTE: If you can't get enough chickpea water from the jars, substitute with boiling water.

MAKE IT GF: You can use your favourite brand of gluten-free bread for the picada.

Cut the bread into ½cm slices. Heat 1 tablespoon of the oil in a large, wide-bottomed frying pan or casserole dish and add the bread. Fry over a medium heat for 2–3 minutes on each side until well browned, then lower the heat, add the garlic, cumin and paprika and stir-fry for 30 seconds until the spices start to release a little oil.

Transfer the spiced bread to a small blender and add the vinegar, 5 tablespoons of the chickpeas and 200ml of the chickpea water and blitz until you have a thick paste.

Heat the remaining tablespoon of olive oil in the same pan, then add the spinach and stir-fry for 2 minutes until just wilted. Transfer to a bowl, then add the remaining chickpeas and blitzed bread mixture to the pan along with the hot water. Bring to the boil, then simmer for 10 minutes, stirring occasionally, until the sauce has reduced and is just clinging to the chickpeas, or 20 minutes if you are using tinned rather than jarred chickpeas.

Add the spinach, taste and adjust the salt and vinegar as needed, and serve hot with the toast or fried bread, scattered with a pinch of paprika and a drizzle of extra virgin olive oil.

ULTIMATE BEAN CHILLI WITH WALNUTS & CHOCOLATE

Serves: 4 generously   Prep: 15 minutes   Cook: 1 hour

I wasn't sure I'd be able to improve on the ever-popular three bean chilli from *The Green Roasting Tin*, but this version, enriched with walnuts and dark chocolate, is now my go-to recipe. You can freeze extra portions, and next-day leftovers are really excellent topped with potato waffles and grated cheese and then flashed under a hot grill.

2 tablespoons olive oil

1 onion, roughly chopped

250g chestnut mushrooms, roughly chopped

2 cloves garlic, finely grated

2 teaspoons ground cumin

2 teaspoons freshly ground coriander seeds

1–2 teaspoons chipotle chilli flakes

1 heaped teaspoon smoked paprika

100g walnuts, roughly chopped

400ml boiling vegetable stock (gluten-free if required)

1 x 400g tin chopped tomatoes

1 x 400g tin black beans, drained and rinsed

1 x 400g tin kidney beans, drained and rinsed

20g vegan 70% dark chocolate

1 teaspoon brown sugar (optional)

Sea salt flakes, to taste

To serve

Tortilla chips (gluten-free, if required)

Vegan or ordinary sour cream

Sliced avocados

Lime wedges

Fresh coriander leaves

Heat the oil in a large stockpot or your largest saucepan over a medium heat and add the onion, mushrooms and garlic. Cook for 10 minutes, stirring frequently, until softened. Lower the heat, then add the spices. Stir-fry for 30 seconds, then add the walnuts and fry for 5 minutes, stirring frequently.

Add a splash of stock and scrape the base of the pan with a wooden spoon, then add the remaining stock, tomatoes, black beans and kidney beans. Bring to the boil, then lower the heat and simmer for 45 minutes. Add the chocolate and sugar (if using) in the last 5 minutes, then taste and add salt as needed.

Serve in deep bowls with your choice of toppings from the list.

NOTE: My chilli tolerance is low and my chipotle chilli flakes are hot – if you prefer a hotter chilli, add more to taste at the point where you add the other spices.

ALL-IN-ONE SMOKY AUBERGINE & PEPPER TAGINE WITH HALLOUMI CROUTONS

Serves: 4–6   Prep: 15 minutes   Cook: 1 hour 20 minutes (all hands-off)

This is a perfect prep-ahead dish – you can make a batch of it at the beginning of the week for a couple of lunches, then put extra portions in the freezer for a rainy day. It's so warming with the spices and smoky aubergine and requires little more from you than to chop a few ingredients and chuck them in the oven. I'm a bit unorthodox when it comes to spicing tagines – good pre-mixed spice blends like ras el hanout or baharat pack in so much flavour, and you won't need to rummage for lots of spices if you haven't much time on your hands.

2 aubergines, cut roughly
  into 3cm chunks
3 mixed peppers (not green)
  cut into 3cm chunks
1 red onion, roughly chopped
2 tablespoons olive oil
3 tablespoons baharat spice mix
1 teaspoon smoked paprika
2 cloves garlic, finely grated
1 teaspoon sea salt flakes
2 x 400g tins chopped tomatoes
200ml boiling water or vegetable
  stock (gluten-free, if required)
1 x 700g jar haricot beans
  (or 2 x 400g tins haricot beans),
  drained and rinsed
225g halloumi, cut into
  crouton-sized cubes

To serve
Smoked or ordinary sea salt flakes
Drizzle extra virgin olive oil
Handful toasted flaked almonds
Chopped fresh mint
  and/or coriander
Quinoa, couscous or flatbreads
  (gluten-free, if required), to serve

Preheat the oven to 200°C fan/220°C/gas 7. (You'll need to use a fan oven to cook the croutons on another shelf; if not, fry or grill the halloumi croutons instead.)

Mix together the aubergines, peppers, onion, olive oil, baharat, smoked paprika, garlic and salt in a large roasting tin. Transfer to the oven and roast for 40 minutes until the vegetables are just charring around the edges.

Add the tinned tomatoes, water or stock and haricot beans, mix well, then return to the oven for a further 40 minutes to reduce the tomato sauce. Twenty minutes before the tagine is ready, pop the halloumi on a baking tray and transfer to another shelf of the oven to roast.

Once the tagine is ready, taste and adjust the salt as needed, transfer to bowls and drizzle with the extra virgin olive oil. Scatter with the halloumi croutons, flaked almonds and chopped herbs before serving hot, with quinoa, couscous or flatbreads on the side.

FREEZE: This freezes very well – defrost in the fridge overnight and warm through in a pan or in a tin in the oven before adding the toppings.

VEGANISE: Just leave out the halloumi croutons, it's a lovely dish by itself.

MEAL PLANS

Here are some suggested seasonal meal plans, including batch-cooking at the weekend, recipes to make for dinner then take for lunch the next day, along with menu ideas for weekend entertaining (with all-important prep plans).

SUMMER MEAL PLAN

SATURDAY

LUNCH
BATCH COOK

SPANISH-STYLE CHICKPEAS
WITH GARLIC & SPINACH   P. 200

MAKES

2 x portions for lunch
2 x portions boxed for the week

DINNER
BATCH COOK

ONE-TIN PASTA SAUCE WITH AUBERGINES,
TOMATOES, CAPERS & PINE NUTS   P. 196

MAKES

2 x portions for dinner
4 x portions for the freezer

SUNDAY

FRIENDS OVER?

See suggested summer party
menu overleaf

MONDAY

PACKED LUNCH
NO COOK

Saturday's batch-cooked SPANISH-STYLE CHICKPEAS
WITH GARLIC & SPINACH
Serve with nice baguettes

DINNER
LINGUINE WITH COURGETTES, PINE NUTS & CHILLI   P. 38

TUESDAY

DINNER
MINIMUM COOK

Pasta bake made with Saturday's batch-cooked ONE-TIN PASTA
SAUCE WITH AUBERGINES, TOMATO, CAPERS & PINE NUTS
Stir through hot pasta, cover with melted cheese
and breadcrumbs, stick under the grill

WEDNESDAY

DINNER

RETRO-FABULOUS ORANGE, BUTTERBEAN,
ARTICHOKE & OLIVE SALAD (with enough
for lunch tomorrow)   P. 80
Serve with nice bread and butter

THURSDAY

PACKED LUNCH
NO COOK

RETRO-FABULOUS ORANGE, BUTTERBEAN, ARTICHOKE
& OLIVE SALAD serve with nice bread and butter

DINNER
ALL-IN-ONE ORZO WITH BAKED FETA,
TOMATOES & OLIVES   P. 48

FRIDAY

DINNER

CRISP PEA & HALLOUMI FRITTERS
WITH LEMON & HERB MAYONNAISE   P. 124

Option to serve with defrosted SPANISH-STYLE
CHICKPEAS WITH GARLIC & SPINACH

A LIGHT LUNCH OR DINNER PARTY FOR A VERY HOT SUMMER DAY

SERVES 4

CRISPS (I LIKE TORRES TRUFFLE CRISPS)

LOTS OF NICE BREAD AND BUTTER

SIMPLY GRIDDLED COURGETTES
WITH MINT & PARMESAN (VEGANISABLE, GF)   **P. 150**

MARINATED BUTTERBEANS & TOMATOES
WITH PISTACHIO & SPRING ONION PESTO (VG, GF)   **P. 148**

FENNEL WITH BURRATA,
BROAD BEANS & POMEGRANATE (GF)   **P. 132**

WARM MADELEINES WITH
CHOCOLATE SAUCE* AND STRAWBERRIES
(SHOP-BOUGHT, OR SEE *CRUMB* BY RUBY TANDOH)

*Chop 100g 70% dark chocolate and gently heat 200ml single cream in a pan until almost boiling. Add the chopped chocolate and turn off the heat. Whisk until smooth.

PREP PLAN

(approx. 1 hour to cook and prep)

---

* Shave the fennel, get it into a bowl of cold water. Set aside. Take the burrata out of the fridge.

* Slice the tomatoes, grate the garlic, etc. Get them into a pan. Prep the pistachio pesto.

* Put the beans into the tomato pan. Finish the pistachio pesto, turn off the beans. Beans done! Set aside at room temperature.

* Slice the courgettes, oil them, get them on the griddle. Make the parmesan dressing.

* Courgettes done! Set aside at room temperature.

* Cook and pod the broad beans, cut and deseed the pomegranate (or open the packet). Make dressing. Fennel salad done!

* Chop the chocolate for the sauce and set aside.

* Find serving plates for each dish, stick the crisps in bowls, bread on board, butter in a dish. Pour yourself a glass of wine.

* About 15 minutes before everyone arrives, arrange the food in serving dishes.

* Once you're all done with the mains, make the chocolate sauce and slice the strawberries while the madeleines warm through in the oven.

Non-food-related tips

* Chill the wine/craft beers asap in the morning. Stick a nice scented candle on 30 minutes before anyone arrives.

* Get your partner/children/anyone who has arrived unconscionably early to help tidy up/empty the dishwasher/ set the table/mow the lawn. (I have deliberately not asked how the lawnmower works.)

AUTUMN MEAL PLAN

SATURDAY

LUNCH
BATCH COOK

CRISPY LEEK, CHEDDAR
& MUSTARD LOADED POTATOES   P. 186

MAKES

2 x portions for lunch
2 x portions boxed for the week
2 x portions for the freezer

DINNER
BATCH COOK

CRISPY-TOPPED ARTICHOKE, BUTTERNUT SQUASH
& ROSEMARY BAKED GNOCCHI   P. 192

MAKES

2 x portions for dinner
2 x portions boxed for the week
2 x portions for the freezer

SUNDAY

FRIENDS OVER?

See suggested autumn dinner
party menu overleaf

MONDAY

PACKED LUNCH
NO COOK

Sunday's batch-cooked CRISPY LEEK, CHEDDAR
& MUSTARD LOADED POTATOES

DINNER
NO COOK

Sunday's batch-cooked CRISPY TOPPED ARTICHOKE,
BUTTERNUT SQUASH & ROSEMARY BAKED GNOCCHI

TUESDAY

DINNER

ORECCHIETTE WITH CHICKPEAS, TOMATO
& ROSEMARY (with enough for lunch tomorrow)   P. 78

WEDNESDAY

PACKED LUNCH
NO COOK

ORECCHIETTE WITH CHICKPEAS, TOMATO & ROSEMARY

DINNER

30-MINUTE MUSHROOM, PEPPER & BLACK BEAN CHILLI   P. 104

THURSDAY

DINNER

BLACK BEAN NOODLES
WITH MUSHROOMS & PAK CHOI   P. 36

FRIDAY

DINNER

20-MINUTE CRISP-TOPPED BROCCOLI
& CAULIFLOWER MAC & CHEESE   P. 58

A WARMING AUTUMNAL DINNER PARTY

SERVES 6

CHEESE TWISTS OR CHEESE STRAWS
(SHOP-BOUGHT, OR SEE *INDIA EXPRESS*)

THE BEST CAULIFLOWER SOUP,
WITH CHILLI ALMOND BUTTER (VEGANISABLE, GF) **P. 68**
(SERVE WITH NICE BREAD)

SPICED SLOW-COOKED MUSHROOM PIE
WITH CELERIAC & CHEDDAR MASH
(VEGANISABLE, GF) **P. 160**

BROCCOLI, DATE, PECAN
& CHILLI CHOPPED SALAD (VG, GF) **P. 84**

SHOP-BOUGHT CHOCOLATE PUDDINGS OR HOMEMADE
CHOCOLATE BREAD AND BUTTER PUDDING, ICE CREAM
(SEE *THE SWEET ROASTING TIN* OR DELIA'S *WINTER COLLECTION*)

PREP PLAN

(approx. 2 hours to cook and prep)

* The day before: make the cheese twists / chocolate bread and butter pudding (or just buy both in).

* On the day, prep and cook the mushroom pie filling and topping.

* While the mushrooms and celeriac are in the oven, simmer the cauliflower for the soup, make the chilli almond butter, then blitz the soup.

* Mash the celeriac topping, assemble the mushroom and celeriac pie and grill. If serving within the hour, leave to one side and reheat at 160°C fan/180°C/gas 4 for 10–15 minutes before serving hot. If serving after an hour, refrigerate once cool, then reheat for 20 minutes in the oven until piping hot all the way through.

* Once you're done with the pie, chop all the ingredients for the broccoli and date salad, assemble and set aside. If serving within a couple of hours, mix the dressing through, otherwise keep the dressing to one side, refrigerate all the chopped elements, and mix together half an hour before serving.

* Slice the bread, pop the butter in a dish, stack your soup bowls and serving plates on the side ready to warm in a low oven. Find a serving platter for the salad.

* Have a sit down, if possible, before your guests arrive. See non-food-related tips on page 213 for tasks to delegate.

WINTER MEAL PLAN

LUNCH
BATCH COOK

ULTIMATE BEAN CHILLI
WITH WALNUTS & CHOCOLATE   P. 202

MAKES

2 x generous portions for lunch
2 x generous portions boxed for the week

DINNER
BATCH COOK

SLOW-COOKED ROSEMARY & RED WINE
MUSHROOM RAGU   P. 194

MAKES

2 x portions for dinner
4 x portions for the freezer

SUNDAY

FRIENDS OVER?

See suggested winter entertaining
menu overleaf

MONDAY

PACKED LUNCH
NO COOK   -

Saturday's batch-cooked ULTIMATE BEAN CHILLI WITH WALNUTS
& CHOCOLATE

DINNER

ROASTED TOFU & AUBERGINE WITH CHILLI-PEANUT
SATAY SAUCE   P. 52

TUESDAY

DINNER
NO COOK

Saturday's batch-cooked SLOW-COOKED ROSEMARY & RED
WINE MUSHROOM RAGU
(If you wish, stir the defrosted sauce and cooked pasta together,
cover with cheese and breadcrumbs and bake for a pasta bake)

WEDNESDAY

DINNER

CRISPY MASALA CHICKPEAS, LEMON DAL
& PITTA CHIPS (with enough for lunch tomorrow)   P. 70

THURSDAY

PACKED LUNCH
NO COOK

CRISPY MASALA CHICKPEAS, LEMON DAL & PITTA CHIPS

DINNER

AUBERGINE PARMIGIANA PASTA BAKE   P. 118

FRIDAY

DINNER

MAPO-STYLE TOFU WITH MUSHROOMS,
CHILLI & SPRING ONIONS   P. 56
Serve with shop-bought dumplings, spring rolls, etc.,
for a Friday-night feast

WINTER ENTERTAINING MENU

SERVES 4

**ROSEMARY, CHILLI & BROWN SUGAR
ROASTED NUTS** (VG, GF)   P. 226

**SPICED ROASTED CARROTS & HAZELNUTS
WITH SILKY BUTTERBEAN MASH** (VG, GF)   P. 136

**MISO BARLEY MUSHROOMS
WITH CORIANDER PESTO** (VG)   P. 162

CHEESEBOARD, NICE CRACKERS, DATES, NUTS, ETC.
(TRY PALACE CULTURE CHEESE IF VEGAN)

NOTES: The mushrooms, pearl barley, coriander pesto, carrots and mash will all sit happily in the fridge all day if you prep them in the morning for evening guests, just factor in that they'll need warming up for longer (cover the mushrooms, barley and carrots in foil and warm at 160°C fan/180°C/gas 4 for 15-20 minutes until piping hot). The mash will warm in a pan. Try not to leave the cooked food out at room temperature for more than an hour.

PREP PLAN

(approx. 1 ½ hours to cook and prep)

---

* Prep and start the miso barley mushroom dish – put the pearl barley in the oven, then prep the mushrooms and pop them in the oven too. Make the coriander pesto and set it aside.

* Prep the spiced roasted carrots, then set aside until the mushrooms and pearl barley come out of the oven. Ditto with the nuts and hazelnuts for the carrot topping.

* Make the butterbean mash.

* Once the mushrooms and pearl barley are out of the oven, put the carrots and nuts in on separate shelves. Set timers.

* Assemble your crackers, dates, nuts, etc., for the cheeseboard, arrange the cheese on a board or plate and refrigerate.

* Find and stack your bowls for the starter and plates/bowls for the mains.

* About 5 minutes before serving, warm the nuts through in the oven for 2 minutes.

* Warm the butterbean mash through in a pan until piping hot and reheat the carrots, uncovered, in the oven for 5–6 minutes until hot, then divide between four warmed bowls.

* Pop foil over the pearl barley and mushroom dishes and keep them warm in a low oven while you eat the carrots and butterbean mash. Just before serving, stir half the coriander pesto through the pearl barley, then plate up on four warmed plates with the remaining pesto on top.

* Take the cheeseboard out of the fridge half an hour or so before serving your main, so the cheese can sit at room temperature.

SPRING MEAL PLAN

SATURDAY

LUNCH
BATCH COOK

COCONUT DAL WITH ROASTED SWEET POTATOES
& CHILLI-LIME PICKLED ONIONS   P. 198

MAKES

2 x portions for lunch
2 x portions boxed for the week
2 x portions for the freezer

DINNER
BATCH COOK

ONE-POT PASTA WITH PEPPERS & HARISSA   P. 190

MAKES

2 x portions for lunch
2 x portions boxed for the week
1 x portion for the freezer

SUNDAY

FRIENDS OVER?

See suggested spring
menu overleaf

MONDAY

PACKED LUNCH
NO COOK

Saturday's batch-cooked COCONUT DAL WITH ROASTED
SWEET POTATOES & CHILLI-LIME PICKLED ONIONS

DINNER

GRIDDLED ASPARAGUS, BLACK OLIVE
& LEMON POLENTA WITH FETA   P. 40

TUESDAY

DINNER
NO COOK

Saturday's batch-cooked ONE-POT PASTA WITH
PEPPERS & HARISSA

WEDNESDAY

DINNER

LEMONGRASS, TURMERIC & TOFU NOODLES   P. 86
(with enough for lunch tomorrow)

THURSDAY

PACKED LUNCH
NO COOK

LEMONGRASS, TURMERIC & TOFU NOODLES

DINNER

PARMESAN & LEMON TENDERSTEM
WITH GREEN PEA ORZOTTO   P. 62

FRIDAY

DINNER

EVERYDAY CHICKPEA & SPINACH CURRY   P. 110
Serve with yogurt and shop-bought samosas and pakoras
for a Friday-night feast

Option to serve with defrosted COCONUT DAL WITH ROASTED
SWEET POTATOES & CHILLI-LIME PICKLED ONIONS

A NICE SPRING LUNCH OR DINNER MENU

SERVES 4

CRISPY BAKED RAVIOLI
WITH SOUR CREAM & CHIVE DIP   P. 228

LEMONY POLENTA WITH ROASTED CAULIFLOWER,
PINE NUTS, RAISINS & CAPERS (GF)   P. 142

WHOLE-BAKED RICOTTA WITH THYME-ROASTED
JERSEY ROYALS, NEW SEASON ASPARAGUS & LEMON
(GF)   P. 154

GOOD SHOP-BOUGHT ICE CREAM
WITH CRUSHED PEANUT OR SESAME BRITTLE
(SHOP-BOUGHT, OR SEE *INDIA EXPRESS*)

NOTES: Annoyingly, the polenta is best made at the last minute just before serving, but you can mitigate how much of a pain this is by a) thinking about how tasty the dish is and b) keeping all your ingredients weighed out and ready on a tray or plate so you're not scrabbling in cupboards when your friends arrive, realising you have no vegetable stock, etc. etc.

As with the winter menu, try not to leave cooked food out for more than an hour.

PREP PLAN

(approx. 1 ½ hours to cook and prep)

---

* The day before: make the peanut brittle (optional – buy in sesame brittle otherwise).

* On the day, prep and roast the potatoes.

* Prep the asparagus, and prep the cauliflower for the oven.

* Put the asparagus, etc. in the tin with the potatoes and other ingredients, make a space for the ricotta, set aside. You'll pop it in the oven to bake 20 minutes before you want to serve.

* Roast the cauliflower, then set aside. Meanwhile, make the dressing for the cauliflower polenta dish and weigh out/set aside everything you need to make the polenta.

* Drizzle the ravioli with olive oil, season with salt and parmesan, and set aside. Make the sour cream dip or decant the shop-bought dip.

* Pop the ravioli into the oven 5 minutes before you expect your guests to arrive. (If they're late, flash them back in the oven to warm through before serving.)

* While everyone tucks into drinks, crispy ravioli and dip, pop the cauliflower back in the oven to warm up and make the polenta.

* Just before serving the polenta and cauliflower in warmed bowls, upend the ricotta into the potato and asparagus tin and roast for 20 minutes.

* Roughly chop the brittle just before you need it and serve scattered over the ice cream.

ROSEMARY, CHILLI & BROWN SUGAR ROASTED NUTS

Serves: many   Prep: 5 minutes   Cook: 15—20 minutes

These are inspired by Nigella's excellent Union Square Café bar nuts (which were, in turn, inspired by bar snacks she ate in New York) from *Nigella Bites*. I make random variations of them so often that I've stopped looking up a recipe, but I wrote this down so you can recreate them. They're incredible to serve with drinks (even nicer warm) when friends come round, or indeed just to keep in a jar on the counter for walk-through snacking.

300g mixed nuts
2 tablespoons olive oil
3 sprigs rosemary,
   leaves finely chopped
1 teaspoon chilli flakes
1 tablespoon brown sugar
1 teaspoon sea salt flakes

Preheat the oven to 180°C fan/200°C/gas 6. Mix the nuts, olive oil, rosemary, chilli flakes, brown sugar and sea salt flakes in a roasting tin large enough to hold all the nuts in one layer, then transfer to the oven to roast for 15–20 minutes until toasted and fragrant.

Let them cool for 10 minutes, before serving warm or at room temperature. Leftovers can be stored in a jar for up to a week (if they last that long).

CRISPY BAKED RAVIOLI WITH SOUR CREAM & CHIVE DIP

Serves: 4 to share   Prep: 5 minutes   Cook: 12–16 minutes

What's better than shop-bought ravioli? Crispy shop-bought ravioli. A novelty dish, but a fun one to wheel out hot with a glass of something cold (and ideally fizzy) – purists look away, because the sour cream and chive dip really makes this dish. I forgot to scatter parmesan over the ones opposite before baking, but I have included it in the method below so you don't.

250g shop-bought ravioli
   (e.g. spinach and ricotta
   or butternut squash and sage)
1 ½ tablespoons olive oil
Pinch sea salt flakes
Handful grated vegetarian
   parmesan

For the dip
1 x tub shop-bought sour
   cream and chive dip
OR
150ml sour cream
2 tablespoons chopped
   fresh chives
Sea salt flakes, to taste

Preheat the oven to 180°C fan/200°C fan/gas 6. Put the ravioli in a lined roasting tin or baking tray large enough to hold them all in one layer, very gently separating any that are stuck together. Drizzle over the oil, scatter over the salt, then gently mix with your hands so the ravioli are evenly coated.

Scatter with the vegetarian parmesan, then bake for 15 minutes until puffed up like crisp, golden brown planets (check after 12 minutes and return to the oven for a further 3–4 minutes if needed).

Meanwhile, decant the bought dip into a nice dipping bowl or mix together the sour cream and chives in a bowl and season with salt.

Once the ravioli are cooked to your liking, serve within 5 minutes – they're best eaten warm. You can make these in advance, then warm them through in a hot oven just before serving.

VEGAN PARMESAN

Serves: 4 generously   Prep: under 10 minutes

This couldn't be easier to make, and even if you are not dairy-free or vegan, it's a delicious topping for pasta (or eaten straight from the jar with a spoon).

50g blanched hazelnuts
  or pine nuts
½ small clove garlic,
  finely grated
1 teaspoon nutritional yeast
2 teaspoons sea salt flakes,
  plus extra as needed

Tip the nuts, grated garlic, nutritional yeast and sea salt flakes into a high-speed blender. Blitz to a rubble, then taste and adjust the salt if needed. (It should be pretty salty.)

Store whatever you don't use in an airtight container in the fridge for up to 2 days.

EASIEST MICROWAVE (OR STOVETOP) BASMATI RICE

I think most of my books have included this method – my family always cook basmati rice in the microwave (not from packets, but raw rice and water in a bowl). It comes out perfectly every time, with lovely separated grains – perfect in fried rice, or alongside any curry.

Serving size: If your family are big rice eaters, you'll want 300g basmati rice to serve four people. Otherwise, 200g basmati rice will most likely do you for four portions.

To rinse or not to rinse: Mum is evangelical about rinsing rice before cooking, as it gets the starch out along with any impurities. My sister never rinses her rice, and points out that we can never tell the difference. On balance, and with a really good brand like Tilda, I tend not to because the rice comes out 'drier', which I prefer. You decide. Rinsing lentils is, however, mandatory.

IN THE MICROWAVE

To serve 2–4
200g basmati rice, rinsed
   and drained well, if you like
400ml boiling water

To serve 4–6
300g basmati rice, rinsed
   and drained well, if you like
570ml boiling water

You'll need a large Pyrex bowl and a plate that will cover the top of the bowl to act as a nice, snug lid.

Put the rice and boiling water into the bowl, cover with the plate and cook on medium (if your microwave's max power setting is 1000, then you want 800) for 11 minutes (for 200g rice) or 14 minutes (for 300g rice). Leave to stand for 10 minutes.

IN A SAUCEPAN

To serve 2–4

200g basmati rice, rinsed
  and drained well, if you like
400ml water or stock

To serve 4–6

300g basmati rice, rinsed
  and drained well, if you like
600ml water or stock

You will need a saucepan with a tight-fitting lid. If your lid doesn't fit tightly or has a hole in it, use a sheet of foil underneath the lid.

Put the rice and water or stock into the saucepan and bring to the boil, then cover the pan tightly with the lid. Turn the heat right down (I will sometimes move it to a less-fierce gas hob at this point) and let it gently simmer for 13 minutes from the point you put the lid on (for 200g) or 15 minutes (for 300g). Do not open the lid before the appointed cooking time – this way lies disaster. Once cooked, let the saucepan stand with the lid ajar and the heat off for a few minutes. You can spread out the hot cooked rice on a plate to fluff through and help it steam-dry.

FRIDGE

ABOUT THE AUTHOR

RUKMINI IYER is the bestselling author of the *Roasting Tin* series, selling over 1.75 million copies worldwide. They've transformed the cookery space in the UK, leading the one-tin, one-pot and one-pan revolution, and remain firm favourites among fans of maximum-flavour, minimum-hassle cooking. She grew up in Cambridgeshire with the best of three food cultures: Bengali and South Indian food from her parents' Indian heritage, along with classic eighties' mac and cheese, sponge pudding, and cheese and pineapple on a stick.

Rukmini is a columnist for the *Guardian* and BBC *Gardeners' World* magazine, and writes for numerous publications, including BBC *Good Food* magazine, Waitrose and Fortnum & Mason. She strongly believes that making time to eat well – for oneself or for family dinners – is an integral part of the day, and as a new mother with limited time but a good appetite, she's passionate about helping other households cook great, minimum-effort dinners.

When she's not cooking, Rukmini loves gardening, wandering around food markets with Border collie and toddler in tow and entertaining at home with her husband (often friends, more often the baby and dog).

ACKNOWLEDGEMENTS

As always, my thanks to the wonderful team who make the books what they are: Pene Parker for your beautiful design, art direction and friendship; David Loftus for the fantastic photography; Jo Jackson for the food styling and running the food shoots with extraordinary capability and good humour; Tamsin English for your crack editing, asides and general brilliance; and not least to my agent, the amazing Felicity Blunt, for all your invaluable encouragement and support.

Thank you to the whole team at Vintage for your help bringing this book into the world – Hannah Telfer, Marianne Tatepo, Emily Martin, Konrad Kirkham, Graeme Hall and Rowena Skelton-Wallace on the publishing side; Lucie Cuthbertson-Twiggs, Sarah Bennie and Carmella Lowkis on marketing and publicity. And many, many thanks to Clare Sayer, Helena Caldon and Lucy Kingett for the copyedit and proofreading.

Pippa Leon and Jo Jackson, thank you for the incredibly helpful and thorough recipe testing – what would I do without you? Many thanks also to Emma Cantlay, Charlotte Van Holthe and Caitlin MacDonald for your excellent assistance on the food shoot. And to my friends-and-family recipe testing team Christine Beck, Danielle Adams Norenberg, Emma Drage, Laura and John Hutchinson, James Mutton, Rosanna Breckner, Rosanna Downes, Padmini Iyer, Mohit Dalwadi, and Parvati and Vijay Iyer (hi, Mum and Dad!) – your feedback has been invaluable to finalise the recipes, thank you all so much.

At home, I couldn't have written this book without a brilliant team keeping me sane and looking after the baby and house so I could focus on writing and testing – thank you Leidy Jimenez and Boryana Adamova, I couldn't do this without you!

Tim, thank you for being you – the best husband I could ever have wished for. And Alba, darling, this book is for you, even though you would almost always rather eat slivers of fridge-cold butter in lieu of dinner. Which I can't say I entirely disapprove of.

THE ROASTING TIN SERIES

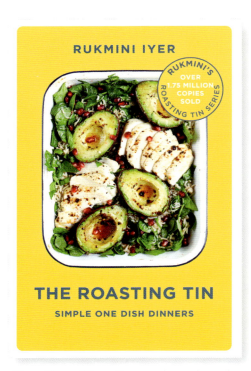

RUKMINI IYER

RUKMINI'S OVER 1.75 MILLION COPIES SOLD ROASTING TIN SERIES

THE ROASTING TIN
SIMPLE ONE DISH DINNERS

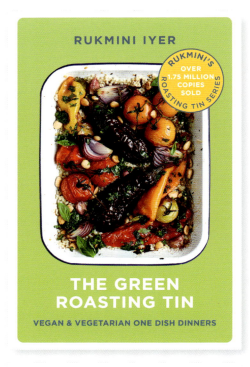

RUKMINI IYER

RUKMINI'S OVER 1.75 MILLION COPIES SOLD ROASTING TIN SERIES

THE GREEN ROASTING TIN
VEGAN & VEGETARIAN ONE DISH DINNERS

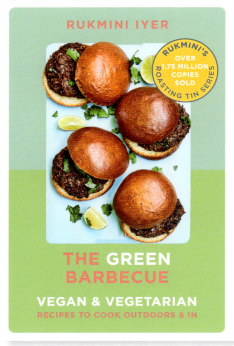

RUKMINI IYER

RUKMINI'S OVER 1.75 MILLION COPIES SOLD ROASTING TIN SERIES

THE GREEN BARBECUE
VEGAN & VEGETARIAN
RECIPES TO COOK OUTDOORS & IN

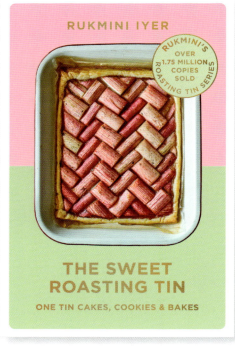

RUKMINI IYER

RUKMINI'S OVER 1.75 MILLION COPIES SOLD ROASTING TIN SERIES

THE SWEET ROASTING TIN
ONE TIN CAKES, COOKIES & BAKES

RUKMINI IYER

RUKMINI'S OVER 1.75 MILLION COPIES SOLD ROASTING TIN SERIES

THE QUICK
ROASTING TIN

30 MINUTE ONE DISH DINNERS

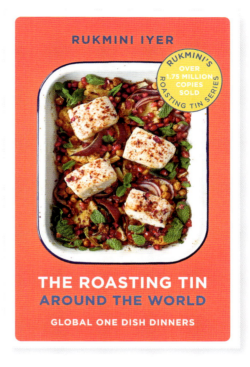

RUKMINI IYER

RUKMINI'S OVER 1.75 MILLION COPIES SOLD ROASTING TIN SERIES

THE ROASTING TIN
AROUND THE WORLD

GLOBAL ONE DISH DINNERS

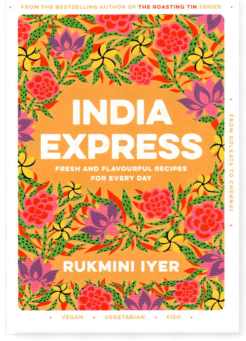

FROM THE BESTSELLING AUTHOR OF THE ROASTING TIN SERIES

INDIA
EXPRESS

FRESH AND FLAVOURFUL RECIPES
FOR EVERY DAY

FROM KOLKATA TO CHENNAI

RUKMINI IYER

VEGAN · VEGETARIAN · FISH

10 9 8 7 6 5 4 3 2 1

Square Peg, an imprint of Vintage,
20 Vauxhall Bridge Road,
London SW1V 2SA

Square Peg is part of the Penguin Random House group
of companies whose addresses can be found at:
global.penguinrandomhouse.com.

First published by Square Peg in 2024
Penguin.co.uk/vintage

A CIP catalogue record for this book is available
from the British Library
ISBN 9781529110449

Art direction, design and prop styling by Pene Parker
Photography by David Loftus
Photography on the back cover, pages 2 and 251
by Emily Marthick, Mindful Chef
Food styling by Jo Jackson and Rukmini Iyer
Food styling assistance by Emma Cantlay, Charlotte Van Holthe
and Caitlin MacDonald
Recipe testing by Pippa Leon and Jo Jackson

Printed and bound in Vietnam.

Penguin Random House is committed to a sustainable future
for our business, our readers and our planet.
This book is made from Forest Stewardship Council® certified paper.